THE ART OF WOODWORKING

PORTABLE
POWER TOOLS

THE ART OF WOODWORKING

PORTABLE POWER TOOLS

TIME-LIFE BOOKS
ALEXANDRIA, VIRGINIA

ST. REMY PRESS
MONTREAL • NEW YORK

THE ART OF WOODWORKING was produced by
ST. REMY PRESS

PUBLISHER	Kenneth Winchester
PRESIDENT	Pierre Léveillé
Series Editor	Pierre Home-Douglas
Series Art Director	Francine Lemieux
Senior Editors	Marc Cassini (Text)
	Heather Mills (Research)
Art Directors	Normand Boudreault, Solange Laberge
Designer.	Luc Germain
Research Editor	Jim McRae
Picture Editor	Christopher Jackson
Writers	Tamsin M. Douglas, Andrew Jones
Contributing Illustrators	Ronald Durepos, Robert Paquet,
	Studio La Perluète Inc.
Administrator	Natalie Watanabe
Production Manager	Michelle Turbide
System Coordinator	Jean-Luc Roy
Photographer	Robert Chartier
Index	Christine M. Jacobs
Proofreader	Judith Yelon

Time-Life Books is a division of Time-Life Inc.,
a wholly owned subsidiary of
THE TIME INC. BOOK COMPANY

TIME-LIFE BOOKS

President	Mary N. Davis
Publisher	Robert H. Smith
Managing Editor	Thomas H. Flaherty
Director of Editorial Resources	Elise D. Ritter-Clough
Associate Publisher	Trevor Lunn
Marketing Director	Regina Hall
Editorial Director	Donia Ann Steele
Consulting Editor	Bob Doyle
Production Manager	Marlene Zack

THE CONSULTANTS

Ted Fuller is the product manager at Delta International Machinery/Porter Cable (Canada). He is currently working in new product development and marketing for woodworking tools and equipment. He is also an amateur woodworker.

Giles Miller-Mead has taught advanced cabinetmaking at Montreal technical schools for more than ten years. A native of New Zealand, he previously worked as a restorer of antique furniture.

Mike O'Malley is a Canadian industrial designer as well as Contributing Editor, Power Tools, for *Woodcuts* magazine .

Joseph Truini is Senior Editor of *Home Mechanix* magazine. A former Shop and Tools Editor of *Popular Mechanics*, he has worked as a cabinetmaker, home improvement contractor and carpenter.

Portable power tools
    p. cm.—(The Art of Woodworking)
Includes index.
ISBN 0-8094-9908-8 (trade)
ISBN 0-8094-9909-6 (lib)
1. Power tools. 2. Woodwork
I. Time- Life Books. II. Series
TT186.P67 1992
684'.083—dc20   92-25558
                                                CIP

For information about any Time-Life book, please call 1-800-621-7026, or write:
Reader Information
Time-Life Customer Service
P.O. Box C-32068
Richmond, Virginia
23261-2068

CONTENTS

John Leeke talks about his
TOOL COLLECTION

I grew up working in my father's cabinetmaking shop. He learned woodworking from an English woodcarver and my early training was in that same tradition with plenty of experience using hand tools such as chisels, planes and saws. Through this work I gained a fundamental knowledge of wood as a material and how to work with it. Since this was a commercial shop, the use of power tools was a natural extension of that training.

In the early 1970s I left my father's shop and began to earn a living on my own. I was interested in the old hand woodworking methods and especially in applying my knowledge of wood in the preservation of historic buildings. I quickly learned that power tools gave me the same results as hand work, but with much less time and effort, leaving me with more time to apply my woodworking skills with hand tools to the details that really matter.

When I began collecting my own set of power tools the first things I bought were a ⅜-inch drill and a saber saw. Later I added a 3-by-21 belt sander and a router to my kit, and—eventually—an 8-inch circular saw. These tools had all-aluminum housings that were bright and shiny when new. They were weighty and substantial tools that you just knew could stand a lifetime of wear and use. And, with regular maintenance and occasional repairs, they have. I still use those same tools in my shop, although the shiny polish has worn to a dull grey.

As time passed, manufacturers began to offer power tools with plastic housings. At first I didn't think much of them and credited myself with having bought my tools back when they were still made of good solid metal. Slowly, however, I began to realize that the plastic housing's lighter design makes a lot of sense when you're using the tools all day long. So I bought another circular saw—this one with a plastic housing.

And then came cordless tools. At first they were unreliable. It took more time fiddling with near-dead batteries and recharging than it did to just stretch out an extension cord and use the old ones. But, as the electronics of the chargers improved and battery technology developed, these handy tools began to save enough time to increase productivity. Now, I have a cordless drill, sander and right-angle grinder.

Something to keep in mind: While these tools allow you to work faster, they also allow accidents to happen a lot quicker. It doesn't take much more than one stroke of a hand saw to know you are cutting yourself. But a power saw can cut off a finger in less than a tenth of a second—before you even realize that something's going wrong. You have to be careful.

John Leeke works as a preservation consultant, helping home-owners, architects and contractors maintain and understand their historic buildings. He lives in Sanford, Maine.

Jan Hoffman discusses
THE SABER SAW

I design and build Pennsylvania-German folk furniture. The inspiration for my work comes from the people who lived and farmed around this region during the 18th and 19th Centuries. They produced utilitarian furniture that was colorfully painted and wonderfully scrolled. The elaborateness of that scrollwork has prompted at least one wag to suggest that the Pennsylvania Germans seemed incapable of cutting anything in a straight line.

When I first expressed an interest in working with wood, my father gave me a 30-year-old table saw and a circular saw of about the same vintage. They were followed shortly by a drill and a good-quality saber saw. For years, these machines—plus a box full of old wooden hand planes—were the extent of my tool inventory.

In the beginning, I used the saber saw only rarely. But I learned to appreciate the value of this much-overlooked tool. Some woodworkers seem to think that bigger means better. They equate the size of the machine and the hum it makes with its productivity. For me, the saber saw proves that is not a valid equation.

My saw comes in handy for everything from cleaning out the rectangular mortises in bench tops to sawing triangular spoon slots in the shelves of cupboards. But where the tool really excels is in cutting the intricate scroll designs in the large side panels of open kitchen dressers or in the pieces of furniture known as bucket benches. Those are the things people used to leave out on the back porch to hold the buckets for bringing in water from the well. If I tried to use a band saw, the whole operation would become very cumbersome, requiring a lot of maneuvering or flipping of the stock. With the saber saw, the wood remains stationary while I simply pivot the tool.

Some woodworkers might choose the band saw if they could only take one machine to a desert island. I'd reach for my saber saw instead.

Jan Hoffman has owned a cabinetmaking shop for the last 10 years. Proud of her Pennsylvania-German lineage, she lives in East Berlin, Pennsylvania.

Bob Jardinico on

NEW TOOL TECHNOLOGIES

E ver since I built my first tree house 30 years ago, I've been fascinated by wood-working. Nowadays, I specialize in reproducing period furniture.

As my skills have improved over the years, so have the demands I place on my tools. To benefit from ever-changing technologies, I have continually updated my inventory of power tools in three main areas: routers, sanders and plate joiners.

I use two routers frequently: a variable speed ½-inch plunge router and a tilting base laminate trimmer. The plunge router is ideal for mortising. With its three depth stops, I can repeat the same three setups over and over. I also use this model to rough out unusual period moldings with a combination of straight and core box bits. Its new variable-speed feature allows me to reduce bit speed to safely use large-diameter panel-raising and multiple-profile bits. With the trimming router, I can cut into a surface at any angle—a useful feature for making undercut moldings. It's also a nice way to gain more flexibility from commonly available bits.

I've recently incorporated two new advances in sanding into my shop. The first is a sanding frame for the belt sander. This rectangular accessory supports the sander, keeping it from tipping and gouging the workpiece. The frame is indispensable for leveling glued-up panels quickly, a process that used to take hours with a hand plane. It's also great for sanding edging strips flush with a plywood panel. The second innovation is the oscillating triangular pad sander. It will finish-sand elaborate shapes and inside corners without marring adjacent surfaces. Equipped with a dust collection system, it not only makes sanding a less unpleasant chore; it also keeps the paper from clogging, cutting down substantially on sanding time.

Plate joiners are essential in my shop. Like many other woodworkers, I bought a basic plate joiner for just one project, then discovered how versatile the tool is. I use plate joints for all the panels I glue up; the biscuits even align slightly warped boards, resulting in a flatter panel. I often substitute plate joints for other joints because, in many cases, they are stronger and less likely to fail as the wood moves in response to changes in humidity.

Bob Jardinico manages woodworking sales for Colonial Saw, a machinery sales and service company based in Massachusetts. He also restores antique furniture in his home workshop in Plymouth, Mass.

CIRCULAR SAW

Riding along the edge of a commercial jig, a circular saw can make a miter cut at a precise angle. The jig ensures that the blade keeps to the intended cutting path.

Traditionally thought of as only a carpenter's tool, the circular saw has earned an important place in the woodworking shop. It is the ideal cutting tool for reducing large panels or long boards to a manageable size. Accordingly, the circular saw is often the first tool woodworkers reach for when they are working with heavy or unwieldy stock.

Imagine trying to rip a 4-by-8 panel of ¾-inch plywood in half on a radial arm saw or crosscutting 10-foot-long planks of 2-by-6 hardwood into 24-inch lengths on a table saw. Both cuts are certainly feasible, but in the time that it would take to set up the cuts and wrestle the wood onto the saw table, the circular saw could have already done the job. The only limitation is that you have to expect its cuts to be relatively inaccurate, compared to the precise results that a well-tuned stationary saw can deliver. However, in the first stages of a woodworking project, you are usually only cutting stock to rough length and width. It is only later, when the pieces have been reduced to a workable size, that you will cut them to their final dimensions.

Still, do not think of the circular saw as strictly a rough cut-off tool. With a plywood blade on its arbor, the saw can make quick work of crosscutting a plywood or hardboard panel without splintering the edges *(page 24)*. An edge guide will make a big difference, improving the accuracy of both rip cuts and crosscuts. Shop-made jigs and accessories will also help guide the saw for miter and taper cuts, and most saws have a built-in adjustment that tilts the base plate for bevel cuts. If you wish to make dadoes or grooves, a circular saw can cut away most of the waste *(page 29)* in less time than it would take to install a dado head on a table or radial arm saw. The job can then be finished with a chisel. Portable power saws can also make plunge cuts *(page 30)*, an operation beyond the scope of any stationary saw.

Circular saws are designated according to their blade diameter. Models range from 4 to 16 inches, but the 7 ¼- and 8 ¼-inch sizes are the most popular home workshop saws. Some woodworkers prefer the smaller 5 ½- and 6-inch saws. Apart from being less expensive than the larger models, these compact tools are lightweight and easy to use. They also usually have the blade on the left-hand side of the motor, making the cutting line easier to see.

Power is another factor that distinguishes one model from another. The bigger the motor, the longer a circular saw will cut without stalling or overheating. If you plan to use the tool principally on hardwood, a saw with a higher horsepower or ampere rating is probably your best bet.

Even with its blade tilted to create a bevel, this 7 ¼-inch circular saw cuts deep to saw through 1-inch-thick stock.

ANATOMY OF A CIRCULAR SAW

There are approximately 40 million portable circular saws in the United States. They vary widely in their design, but all models share certain common features; most importantly, they are powered by a motor connected to an arbor assembly that turns a blade counterclockwise. Depending on the height or angle of the base plate relative to the blade, a saw can be set to cut stock of different thicknesses at a variety of angles between 45° and 90°.

When shopping for a circular saw, keep several factors in mind. Most tools range in horsepower from ½ to 2 ½ h.p. Get a saw with at least 1 horsepower. For the sake of convenience, the tool should have a comfortable handle and a balanced design. Make sure that the depth-of-cut and bevel settings are easy to adjust and that the saw has a large, stable base plate with both a long straight edge and a precise tilting mechanism. For safety's sake, select a saw that features a lock-off switch that must be depressed along with the trigger to turn on the tool. This will prevent accidental startup of the motor.

There are two main designs available for setting a circular saw's depth of cut. On pivot-foot saws, like the model shown on page 15, the tool swivels up or down from a point at the front of the base plate. The angle of the handle changes with the depth of cut. On drop-foot saws, the motor and blade housings are raised or lowered straight up or down relative to the base plate. The angle of the handle remains constant, a feature many users find convenient.

While the 7 ¼-inch saw shown here at right has been the traditional choice of most woodworkers because of its generous depth-of-cut capacity—2 ⅜ inches— the compact 6-inch model at left can also slice through a 2-by-4 at both 90° and 45°.

CIRCULAR SAW SAFETY TIPS

• Avoid steadying a workpiece by hand or propping it on your knee; always clamp stock to a work surface or sawhorses. If the blade binds during a cut, kickback can hurl the workpiece back toward you unless it is securely supported.

• To keep a panel from sagging in the middle and causing the blade to bind, support it all along its length on a platform of 2-by-4s.

• Unplug the saw before changing the blade or making any other adjustments.

• Do not use the saw if either blade guard is missing or damaged; keep the tool clean to ensure that the guards remain in good working order.

• Do not use a saw with parts that are loose or damaged.

• Keep the power cord out of the saw's cutting path.

• Maintain a comfortable, balanced stance when cutting; avoid overreaching.

• Always wear safety glasses when operating the saw; because it cuts on the upstroke, the blade produces a shower of wood chips.

• Keep your hands away from the underside of the base plate when the blade is spinning; whenever possible, keep both hands on the saw throughout a cutting operation.

• Make sure the blade is not in contact with the workpiece when you turn on the saw. Allow the blade to come to full speed before feeding it into the stock.

• Do not force the saw through a cut; allow the blade to cut at its own speed.

• If the blade binds during a cut, do not lift the saw out of the kerf. First, turn the saw off, back the blade up slowly and allow it to stop spinning.

• Make sure that the lower blade guard springs back over the blade at the end of a cut before setting the saw down.

• Do not attempt to cut through nails; this can cause kickback and ruin a blade.

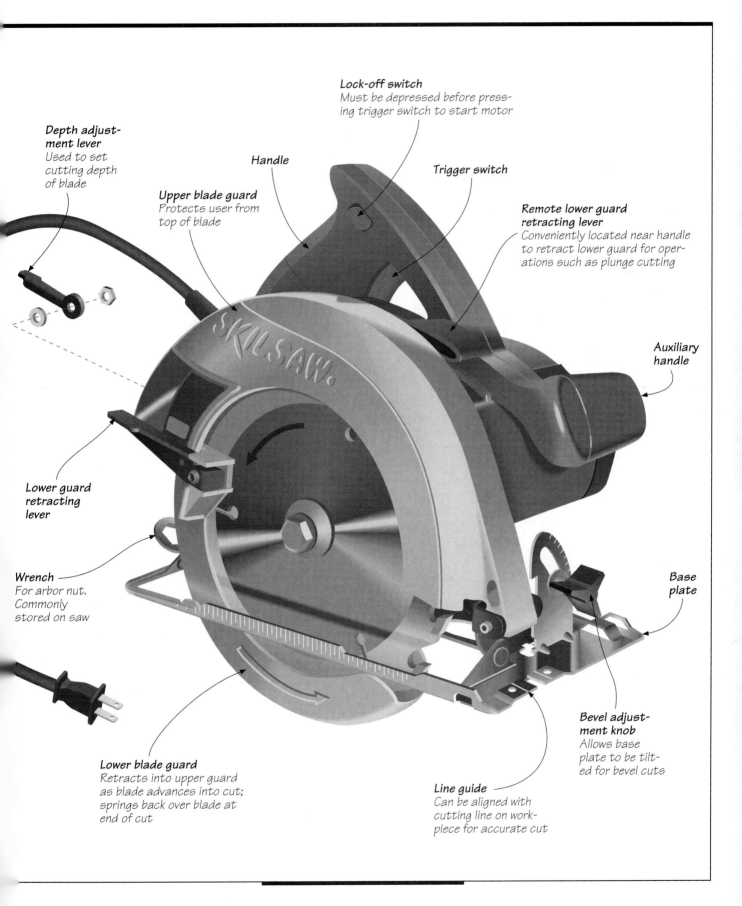

Lock-off switch
Must be depressed before pressing trigger switch to start motor

Depth adjustment lever
Used to set cutting depth of blade

Handle

Trigger switch

Upper blade guard
Protects user from top of blade

Remote lower guard retracting lever
Conveniently located near handle to retract lower guard for operations such as plunge cutting

Auxiliary handle

Lower guard retracting lever

Wrench
For arbor nut. Commonly stored on saw

Base plate

Lower blade guard
Retracts into upper guard as blade advances into cut; springs back over blade at end of cut

Line guide
Can be aligned with cutting line on workpiece for accurate cut

Bevel adjustment knob
Allows base plate to be tilted for bevel cuts

CIRCULAR SAW BLADES AND ACCESSORIES

With the dozens of specialty blades on the market it is entirely possible to transform a circular saw from a job site workhorse into a precision cutting tool. Equipped with a standard combination blade and ones designed to cut specific materials, a saw can crosscut and rip accurately through hardwood, softwood or manufactured panels such as plywood.

The cutting ability of a circular saw blade depends on several factors. A blade's hook angle, which determines how much bite it will take, is a key variable. (The angle is formed by the intersection of one line drawn from the tip of a tooth to the center of the arbor hole and one drawn parallel to the tooth's face.) The width of the kerf that the cutting edge creates is also important; so too is the number of teeth per inch (TPI). A 40 TPI crosscut blade will do its job more slowly than a 20 TPI combination blade, for example, but the finer-toothed model will produce a cleaner cut.

Although all of the blade types illustrated below are available in high-speed steel, carbide-tipped models have for years been the first choice of the majority of woodworkers. While they are more expensive than their steel counterparts, carbide-tipped blades are more economical in the long run. The small tips of carbide alloy welded onto the bodies of these blades can be sharpened dozens of times and hold their edge up to 50 times longer than steel blades.

But even carbide-tipped blades dull with extended use. Smoking, burning, off-line cutting and frequent binding are all signs of a blade in need of sharpening. The best way to keep a blade sharp is to choose the right one for the material you are cutting and to avoid cutting into fasteners or accumulations of pitch.

BLADE TYPES

Combination Blade
The blade type usually supplied with the saw; a general-purpose blade for ripping and cross-cutting.

Crosscut Blade
For fast, smooth cuts across the grain; the blade's teeth are sharpened on the face and back, forming sharp cutting points.

Rip Blade
Also known as a framing blade; the large, hooked teeth make it ideal for fast cuts along the grain.

Hollow Ground Planer Blade
For very smooth rip cuts, crosscuts and angle cuts; ideal for precision cabinet work. The blade's body is thinner than the hub and teeth, reducing the chance of binding in the kerf.

Plywood Blade
For smooth cuts in plywood and veneered stock; small, pointed and finely ground teeth help reduce splintering.

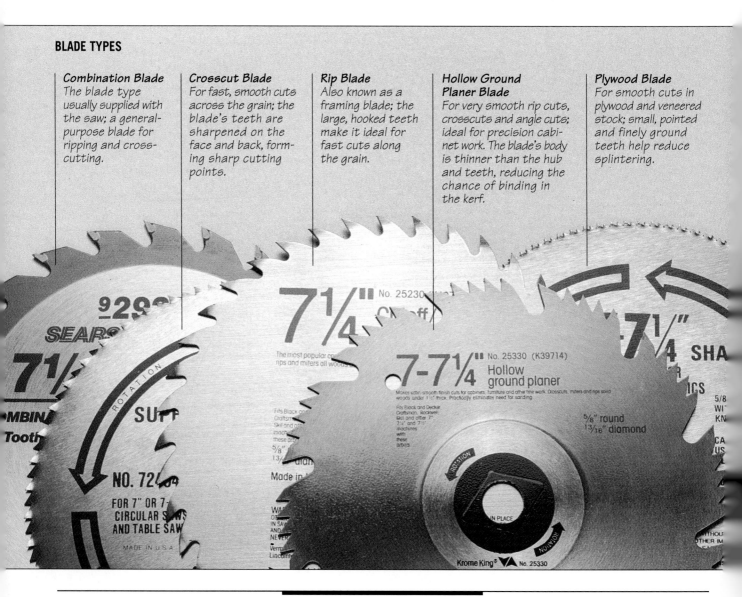

CHANGING A BLADE

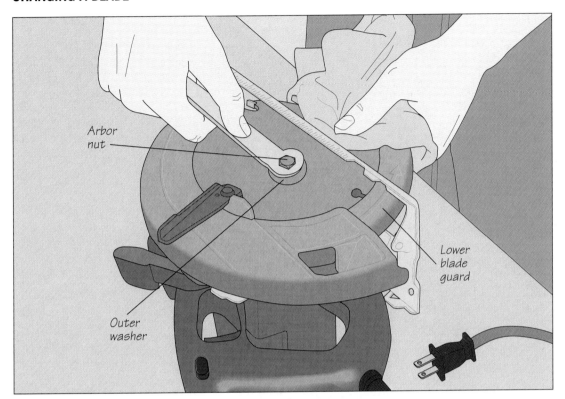

Arbor
nut

Lower
blade
guard

Outer
washer

Removing and installing blades

Unplug the saw, then set it on its side on a work surface with the blade housing facing up. Retract the lower blade guard and, gripping the blade with a rag, loosen the arbor nut with the wrench supplied with the saw *(above)*. Remove the nut and the outer washer, then slide the blade from the arbor. To install a blade, place it on the arbor with its teeth pointing in the direction of blade rotation. Install the washer and the nut, and tighten them by hand. Holding the blade with the rag, use the wrench to give the nut an additional quarter turn. Avoid overtightening.

SHOP TIP

Reference marks for accurate cuts
Some saws do not provide reference marks to help you align the blade with a cutting line on a workpiece; other machines have lines that may not be perfectly aligned for a particular saw blade. Solve the problem by adding your own marks. Cut into a scrap board, then back the saw partly out of the kerf and unplug the machine. Make a mark on the toe of the base plate in line with the kerf, then fix a strip of masking tape on the toe, aligning its edge with the mark. Use the same procedure to make additional marks for angle cuts.

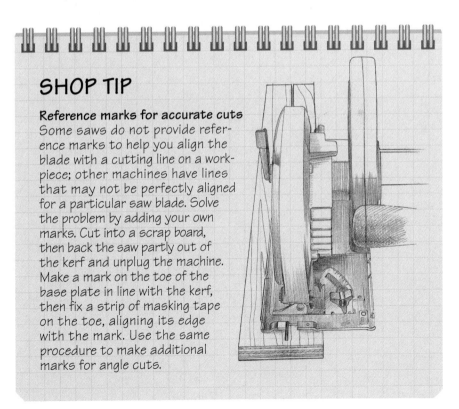

CIRCULAR SAW ACCESSORIES

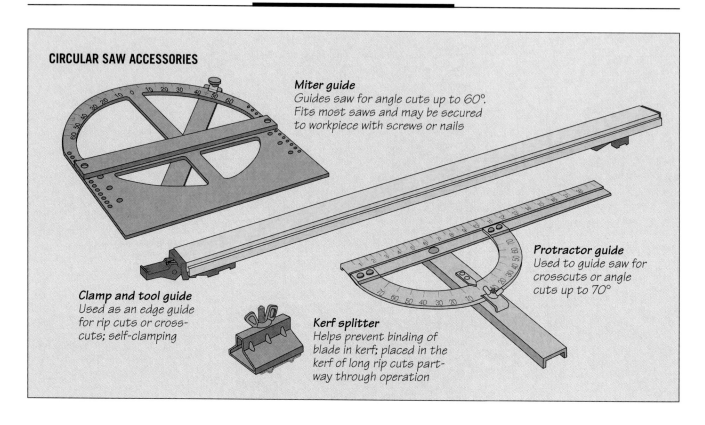

Miter guide
Guides saw for angle cuts up to 60°. Fits most saws and may be secured to workpiece with screws or nails

Protractor guide
Used to guide saw for crosscuts or angle cuts up to 70°

Clamp and tool guide
Used as an edge guide for rip cuts or cross-cuts; self-clamping

Kerf splitter
Helps prevent binding of blade in kerf; placed in the kerf of long rip cuts partway through operation

BUILD IT YOURSELF

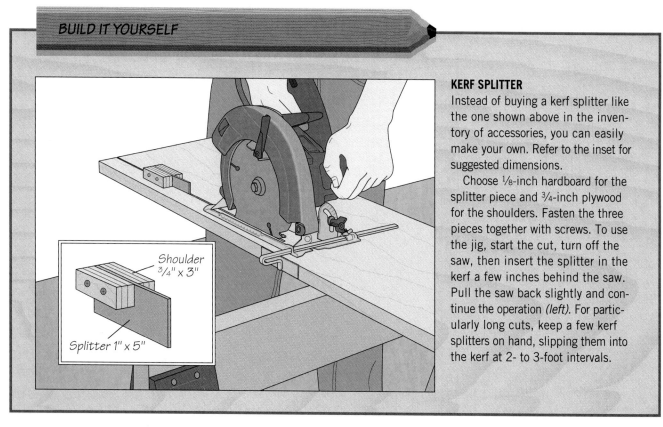

Shoulder
3/4" x 3"

Splitter 1" x 5"

KERF SPLITTER

Instead of buying a kerf splitter like the one shown above in the inventory of accessories, you can easily make your own. Refer to the inset for suggested dimensions.

Choose 1/8-inch hardboard for the splitter piece and 3/4-inch plywood for the shoulders. Fasten the three pieces together with screws. To use the jig, start the cut, turn off the saw, then insert the splitter in the kerf a few inches behind the saw. Pull the saw back slightly and continue the operation *(left)*. For particularly long cuts, keep a few kerf splitters on hand, slipping them into the kerf at 2- to 3-foot intervals.

SQUARING THE BLADE

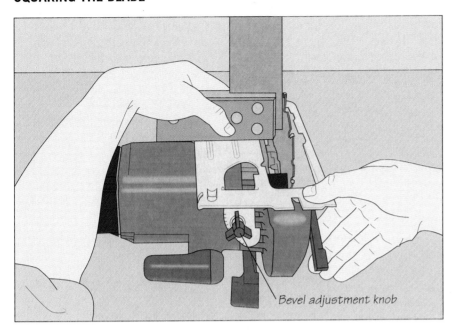

Bevel adjustment knob

Aligning the blade with the base plate
After pulling the plug, set the saw upside down on a work surface with the blade at its maximum cutting depth *(below)*. Retract the lower blade guard, then butt the two sides of a try square against the base plate and the blade between two teeth *(left)*. The square should fit flush against the blade. If there is a gap between the two, loosen the bevel adjustment knob and tilt the base plate until it touches the square, then tighten the knob.

SETTING THE CUTTING DEPTH

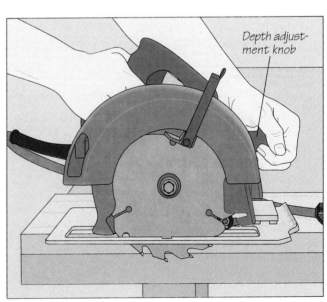

Depth adjust-ment knob

Adjusting blade height
With the saw unplugged, retract the lower blade guard and set the base plate on the workpiece, butting the blade against the edge of the stock. When cutting through a workpiece, set the blade to clear the stock by about ¼-inch. For most blades, one tooth and at least part of the adjoining gullets should project below the workpiece; if not, sawdust will fail to clear the kerf, causing burning. For a pivot-foot saw *(above, left)*, release the depth adjustment lever. Then, keeping the base plate flat on the workpiece, hold the handle and pivot the saw up or down until the blade reaches the correct depth. Tighten the lever. For a drop-foot model *(above, right)*, loosen the depth adjustment knob, then hold the base plate steady as you pull up or press down on the handle. When you have the blade at the depth you need, tighten the knob.

BASIC CUTS

Whether you are crosscutting a narrow board or ripping a sheet of plywood, always protect yourself from kickback by clamping stock to a work surface before cutting it with a circular saw. When applying the clamps, protect the surfaces of the workpiece with wood pads. Other safeguards include keeping saw blades clean, setting the cutting depth no deeper than you need, and making sure that the stock you are cutting is dry and free of any fasteners.

To get accurate results, cut with the blade just to the waste side of the cutting line. Edge guides can also improve precision. Although commercial guides are available in various sizes and at a wide range of prices, a straight board clamped to your workpiece will serve just as well for most jobs.

Since circular saw blades cut on the upstroke, splintering occurs on the visible face of a workpiece. Get in the habit of cutting your stock good face down. If you are working with hardwood or veneered plywood, which has two good faces, score the cutting line with a utility knife before making the cut.

Some commercial guides can be extended up to 8 feet, enabling you to rip a 4-by-8 panel in two. The one shown in this photo is more suitable for crosscutting. It features clamps underneath the guide that secure the device to a workpiece, eliminating the need for separate clamps.

CROSSCUTTING

Cutting stock to length
Clamp the workpiece to sawhorses. Align the blade with the cutting line, then clamp a straightedge guide to the workpiece flush against the saw's base plate. The guide should be longer than the width of the workpiece and square to the edges of the stock. Take care also to set up the clamps so that they will not interfere with the motor as you make the cut. Turn on the saw with the base plate flush against the guide and the blade clear of the stock. Then, gripping the handles firmly with both hands, feed the saw steadily into the workpiece.

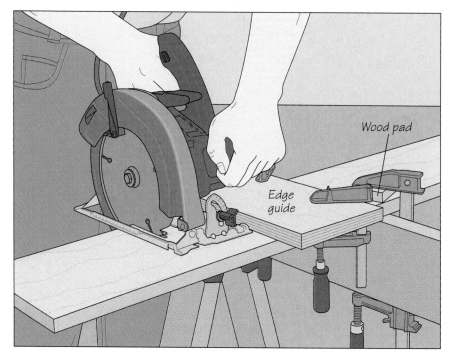

Wood pad

Edge guide

CROSSCUTTING JIG

Simple to make, the shop-built jig shown at right will ensure that your crosscuts are square to the edges of the stock. Select ½-inch plywood for the edge guide and ¾-inch plywood for the fence. The dimensions of the jig depend on the width of the stock you will be cutting and the width of your saw's base plate.

Make the edge guide at least as long as the width of your workpiece and wide enough to clamp to the board without getting in the way of the saw as you are making the cut. The fence should be about 4 inches wide and longer than the combined width of the edge guide and the base plate of the saw. Screw the two parts of the jig together, checking with a try square to make sure that they are perfectly perpendicular.

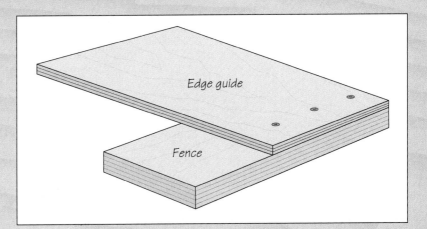

To use the jig, clamp it to the workpiece as you would for a standard crosscut *(page 20)*, making sure the blade is held in alignment with the cutting mark on the workpiece. The fence should always be kept flush against the edge of the workpiece. Run the saw along the edge guide to make the cut. (The first use of the jig will immediately trim the end of the fence flush with the blade.)

For subsequent cuts, clamp the jig to the workpiece, aligning the end of the fence with the cutting mark on your stock.

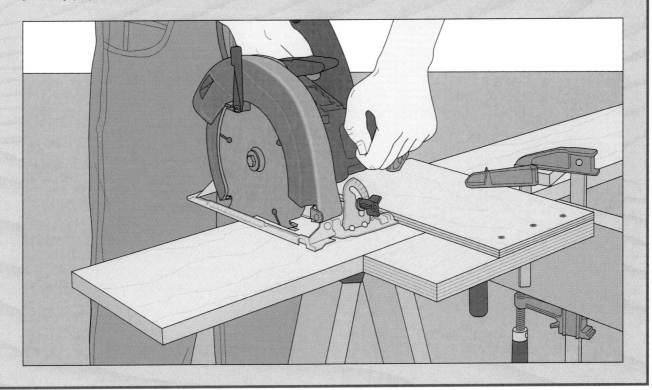

RIPPING

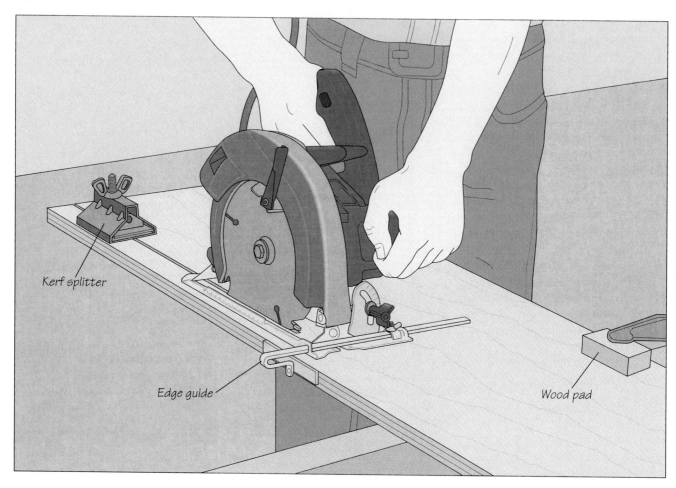

Kerf splitter

Edge guide

Wood pad

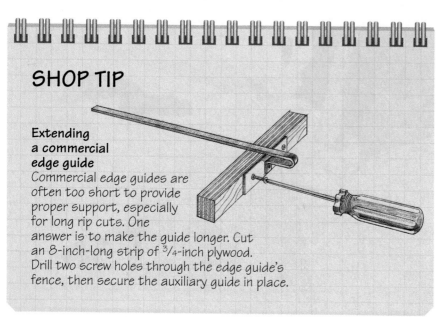

SHOP TIP

Extending a commercial edge guide

Commercial edge guides are often too short to provide proper support, especially for long rip cuts. One answer is to make the guide longer. Cut an 8-inch-long strip of ³/₄-inch plywood. Drill two screw holes through the edge guide's fence, then secure the auxiliary guide in place.

Cutting a long workpiece to width

Install a commercial edge guide on the saw, then align the blade with the cutting line on the board. Butt the edge guide's fence against the edge of the workpiece, then lock it in place. Holding the saw firmly, feed the blade into the board, keeping the edge guide fence flush against the stock. To prevent the blade from binding in a long workpiece, turn off the saw a few inches into the cut and insert a kerf splitter. Pull the saw back a bit, then turn it on and continue the cut.

CUTTING THICK STOCK

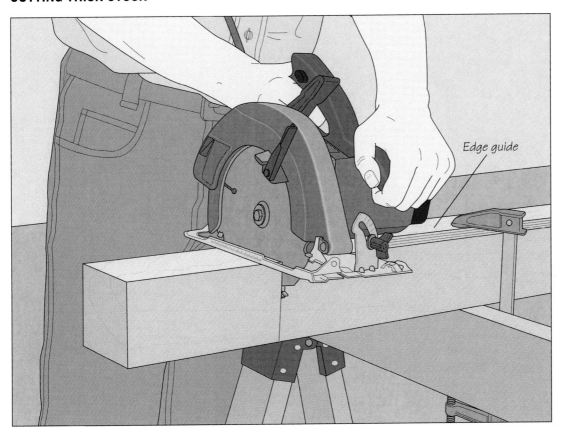

Edge guide

Sawing stock with two intersecting passes
To crosscut stock thicker than the maximum blade depth of your saw, make intersecting cuts from opposite sides of the workpiece. First, mark a cutting line on one face of the stock, then use a try square to extend the line around the other three faces. Set the workpiece on sawhorses and clamp it in position. Align the blade with the cutting line, then butt an edge guide against the saw's base plate and clamp it to the workpiece. Set the cutting depth at slightly more than one-half the thickness of the stock, then make the cut *(above)*. Flip the workpiece over, reposition the clamps and the edge guide, then complete the cut.

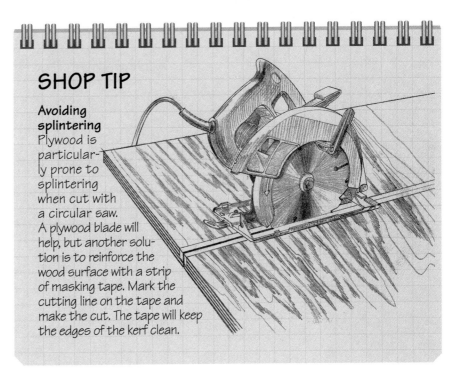

SHOP TIP

Avoiding splintering
Plywood is particularly prone to splintering when cut with a circular saw. A plywood blade will help, but another solution is to reinforce the wood surface with a strip of masking tape. Mark the cutting line on the tape and make the cut. The tape will keep the edges of the kerf clean.

CUTTING LARGE PANELS

Ripping

To prevent a panel from sagging in the middle during a cut and causing the blade to bind, support the stock on a platform of sawhorses and 2-by-4s as shown at left. Make sure that two of the boards will be about 3 inches on either side of the cutting line. Position the panel on the 2-by-4s and clamp it in place. For extra accuracy, clamp a straightedge guide to the panel *(page 25)*. Aligning the blade with the cutting line, cut slowly and steadily while guiding the saw with both hands. Insert kerf splitters as you go to keep the blade from binding.

Crosscutting

Set enough 2-by-4s face up on the shop floor to support the panel at 12-inch intervals; the boards should be a few feet longer than the width of the panel. Position the stock on the boards, shifting two of them to rest about 3 inches on either side of the cutting line. To make the cut, drop to one knee and align the blade with the cutting mark. Gripping the saw with both hands, cut steadily while carefully maintaining your balance *(right)*. As much as possible, keep your weight on the 2-by-4 immediately to the side of the cutting line, rather than on the panel itself.

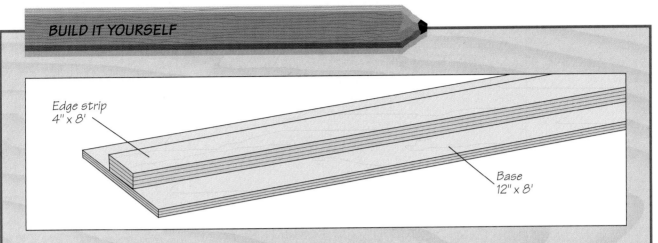

BUILD IT YOURSELF

Edge strip
4" x 8'

Base
12" x 8'

STRAIGHTEDGE GUIDE

The shop-built straightedge guide shown above makes it easy to rip manufactured panels like plywood with great accuracy. Refer to the illustration for suggested dimensions.

Make the base from ¼-inch plywood; use ¾-inch plywood for the edge strip. Glue the strip parallel to the base, offsetting its edge about 4 inches in from one edge of the base. Trim the base to its proper width for your saw by butting the tool's base plate against the jig's edge strip and cutting along the base.

To use the jig, make a cutting mark on the panel, then clamp the stock to a platform of 2-by-4s resting sturdily atop sawhorses. Clamp the guide to the panel, aligning the trimmed edge of the base with the mark on the workpiece.

Make the cut as you would a standard rip cut (page 22), keeping the saw's base plate flush against the edge strip throughout the operation.

SHOP TIP

Carrying large panels
Plywood, particleboard and hardboard panels, particularly 4-by-8s and longer, can be heavy and awkward to carry. A sling fashioned from rope will make the load easier to bear. To make such a sling, tie together the ends of a 20-foot-length of light ½-inch rope. With the panel flat on the floor, loop the rope around two adjacent corners and gather the two strands near the middle, wrapping them with duct tape to form a handle. Hold onto the tape as you gather the panel up under your arm.

MAKING ANGLE CUTS

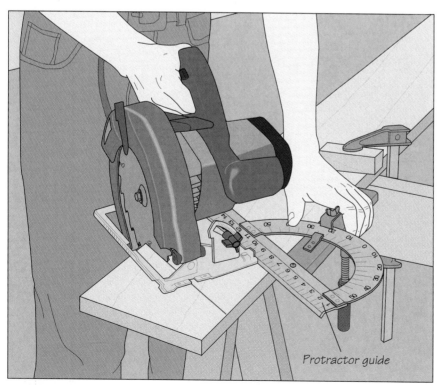

Protractor guide

Using a guide to cut miters
Clamp the workpiece to sawhorses, then set a protractor guide or a miter guide to the angle you wish to cut. Align the saw blade with the cutting line on the workpiece. Place the protractor on the stock, holding its guiding edge against the saw's base plate and its fence against the edge of the workpiece. Grasp the saw and the guide firmly while you are making the cut.

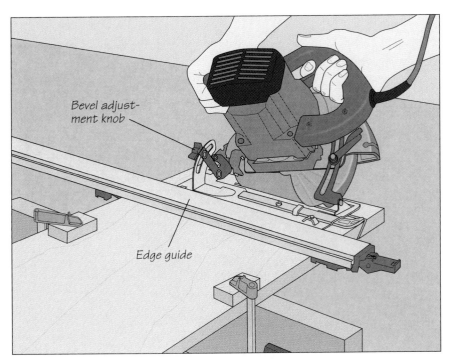

Bevel adjust-ment knob

Edge guide

Making a bevel cut

Loosen the bevel adjustment knob on the saw and set the blade to the desired angle, then tighten the knob. Clamp the workpiece to sawhorses, making sure that nothing will be in the way of the blade during the cut. Align the blade with the cutting mark, then butt an edge guide flush against the saw's base plate. Clamp the guide to the board. Make the cut as you would a standard crosscut, holding the saw firmly with both hands and keeping the base plate flat on the workpiece.

Cutting a taper

Set the stock on a work surface with the cutting line extending several inches off the edge. Position the workpiece so that you will be able to start the cut at the end of the board, rather than on its edge. Line up the blade with the cutting mark, then clamp an edge guide on top of the stock flush against the saw's base plate; measure, if necessary, to make sure that the guide is parallel to the line. Make the cut as you would a standard rip cut. Keep a firm hold on the saw, especially near the end of the cut, when the waste section supporting the tool becomes progressively narrower.

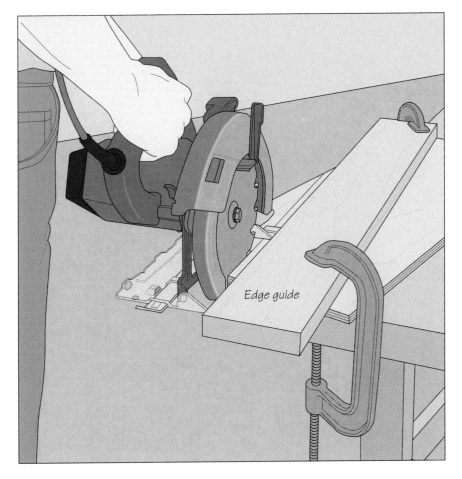

Edge guide

MITER AND CROSSCUTTING GUIDE

For a multipurpose edge guide that is helpful in making either 45° miter cuts or crosscuts, try the jig shown at right. It can be made from a piece of ¾-inch plywood. Refer to the illustration for suggested dimensions.

Cut a triangle with one 90° angle and two 45° angles. (To make a jig for 30° or 60° angles, the sides should be 12, 16 and 20 inches—or any other variation with a 3-4-5 ratio.) Screw the fences to the base, one on each side, opposite one of the 45° angles. The fences must be flush with the edge of the jig base.

To use the jig for a miter cut, first clamp the workpiece to sawhorses. Then align the blade of the saw with the cutting line on the stock and butt the long side of the jig against the saw's base plate. The fence on the bottom of the guide will need to be flush against the workpiece. Clamp the jig in place, and make the cut as you would a standard miter. Keep the saw flush against the jig throughout the operation.

To make a crosscut, use the other side of the jig as your guide.

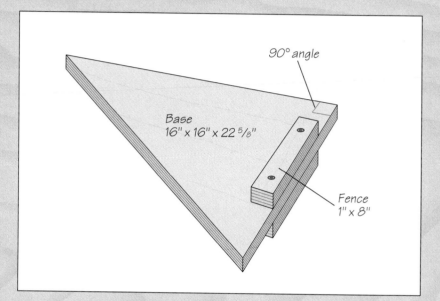

90° angle

Base
16" × 16" × 22 ⁵⁄₈"

Fence
1" × 8"

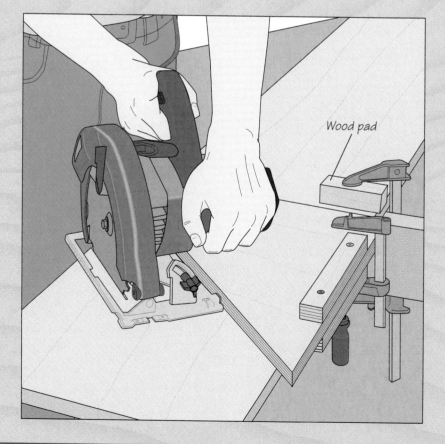

Wood pad

ADVANCED CUTS

A little ingenuity—along with the appropriate jigs and setups—can greatly expand the versatility of a circular saw. Although the tool is not a substitute for a table saw or radial arm saw, it can do much more than simple dimensioning of stock.

When it is inconvenient to use a larger stationary saw, you can call on your portable tool to cut some of the joints for cabinetmaking projects, for instance. Dadoes, rabbets and miters can be formed with precision approaching that of a stationary saw. For cleaner results and less tearout, use a fine-tooth blade when performing such tasks.

Although the circular saw may not always cut wood as quickly as the table saw or radial arm saw, the tool's portability allows it to work in places that are off limits to the stationary machines. The saw can plunge into the middle of a panel, for example, cutting a rectangular hole out of it while leaving the edges intact *(page 30)*. You can also saw arcs or circles by making a series of tangent cuts.

CUTTING DADOES

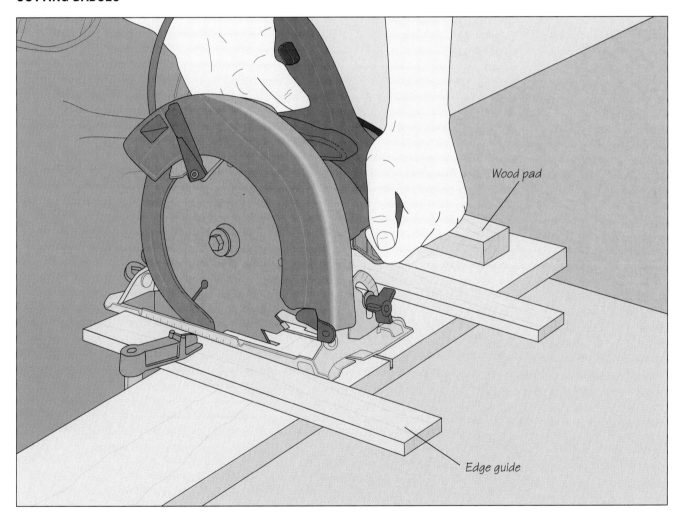

Wood pad

Edge guide

1 Cutting kerfs within the dado outline
Mark the width of the dado on the face of the stock, then clamp it to a work surface. Mark a depth line on the edge of the workpiece as a reference point and set the cutting depth of the blade appropriately for the dado you are making *(page 19)*. Align the blade with one of the width marks and clamp an edge guide in place to keep the saw from cutting beyond that mark. Repeat for the other side of the dado. Gripping the saw firmly, ride the base plate along one guide to cut an edge of the dado. Then run the saw along the second support to cut the channel's other edge *(above)*. To remove as much waste as possible, saw a number of kerfs between the two cuts, working at roughly ⅛-inch intervals.

2 Chiseling out the waste

Holding a wood chisel at a slight angle as shown, strike the handle with a wooden mallet to split off the ridges between the edges of the dado *(left)*. Make sure that the beveled side of the chisel is facing up. After the bulk of the waste has been removed, pare away at the bottom of the dado until it is smooth and even.

MAKING A PLUNGE CUT

1 Biting into the stock

Clamp the workpiece to sawhorses and align the blade with one of the cutting lines. Then clamp an edge guide to the workpiece flush against the base plate of the saw. Make the guide longer than the cutting mark and high enough to guide the saw when it is tilted up. Retracting the lower blade guard with one hand and gripping the handle firmly with the other, rest the toe of the base plate on the workpiece and pivot the saw forward to raise the blade completely clear of the stock. With the back of the blade directly above the start of the cutting line, turn on the saw and slowly lower the cutting edge into the stock *(right)*, keeping the base plate flush against the edge guide. Once the saw is flat on the workpiece, release the blade guard and push the tool forward. When the blade reaches the end of the cutting line, turn off the saw, let the blade stop, and pivot the tool forward to lift it out of the kerf. Make plunge cuts along the three remaining cutting lines, repositioning the edge guide as necessary.

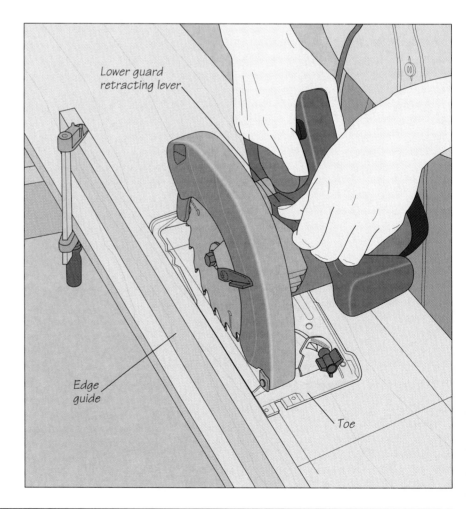

Lower guard retracting lever

Edge guide

Toe

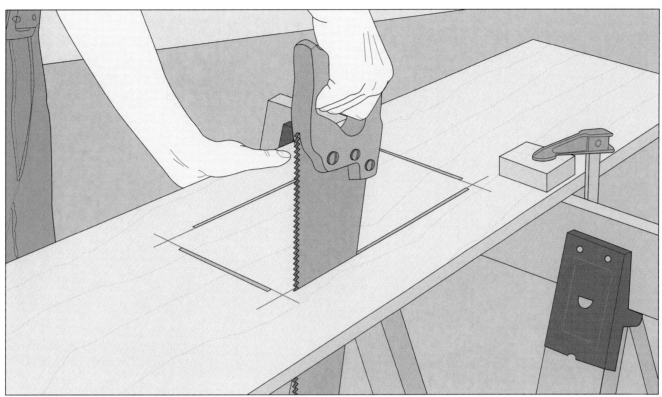

SHOP TIP

Reducing plunge cut splintering
Letting the waste piece sag and finally fall to the shop floor when the last cut detaches it from your workpiece invariably results in splintering of the cut edges. Get cleaner plunge cuts by laying a board across the stock and nailing it to the waste piece before making the final cut. You can then lift out the waste piece without marring the edges of the cutout.

2 **Completing the plunge cut**
Because of its circular blade, a portable power saw will leave a small amount of waste at the beginning and end of each plunge cut. Square the corners with a saber saw *(page 32)* or a hand saw, making sure that you keep the blade vertical as you cut.

SABER SAW

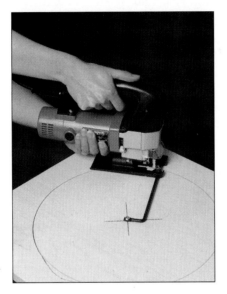

With the help of a commercial circle-cutting jig, a saber saw completes a perfect 360° cut in a piece of ¾-inch plywood. To reduce splintering on the outside surface of the stock, this piece was clamped with its best face down.

The saber saw is often likened to its larger shop cousin, the band saw. Although few woodworkers would consider using the portable tool to resaw a hardwood plank or carve out a cabriole leg, the comparison is apt in other ways. With its relatively narrow blade, the saber saw makes straight and curved cuts with equal ease and accuracy. Aided by commercial or shop-made jigs, it can carve out a perfect circle. And like the band saw, the saber saw can be set up to cut identical copies of a curved pattern.

In certain situations, a portable saw may even be a better choice than its stationary counterpart. If you are working with a long board or wide panel that might require a time-consuming setup on a saw table, it is sometimes simpler to carry the saber saw to the work for a quick cut. Because one end of the blade is free, the cutting edge can be plunged into a workpiece for interior cuts on which a band saw would have to begin at the edge of the stock (page 44).

The saber saw has come a long way since its introduction. Woodworkers complained that the first generation of saws were plagued by inconsistent motor speeds and blades that tended to bend, making it difficult to follow a cutting line. The newest models feature electronic motors that can maintain a constant speed under changing load conditions. And blade manufacturers offer a wide variety of sturdy blades suitable for any situation.

Making precise, splinter-free cuts requires attention to several factors. A key variable is choosing the best blade for the job at hand (page 36). For straight and angled cuts, an edge guide will be of great assistance in keeping the blade in line. Since the saber saw blade cuts on the upstroke, there is a tendency for splintering to occur on the top face of a workpiece. One way to counteract this problem is to slow the rate at which you make the cut. And remember to buff the bottom of your saw's base plate occasionally with steel wool to remove dirt, grime and burrs that could scratch the workpiece.

There is no prescribed way to grip a saber saw. The manner in which you handle the tool will depend on the design of your particular model. Many cuts can be performed with one hand on the handle squeezing the trigger, while the other hand is set on the workpiece safely away from the blade. Other woodworkers prefer to keep both hands on the saw: one on the handle and the other wrapped around the front of the body or barrel of the tool.

The saber saw's unique design allows the blade to be plunged into a workpiece at any point along a cutting line. Resting the base plate flat on the stock during the cut keeps the blade square and will yield clean edges.

ANATOMY OF A SABER SAW

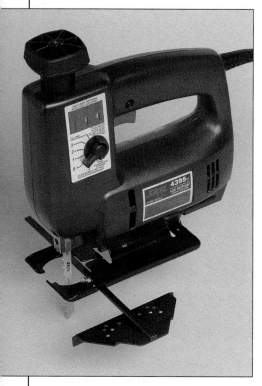

On this scrolling saw, the blade can be rotated 360° by either turning a knob on top of the saw body or by applying simple hand pressure.

All saber saws convert the rotary action of an electric motor into the up-and-down movement of a blade, designed to cut on the upstroke. Tool manufacturers offer three variations on this basic principle. On reciprocating-action machines—once, the standard for saber saws—the blade moves straight up and down. On orbital-action saws—now the most common variety—the blade moves slightly forward on the upstroke, then draws away on the downstroke. Many models, like the one shown opposite, feature both options, permitting you to choose either reciprocating or orbital blade movement.

Orbital-action cutting was developed to make saber saws work more efficiently. By moving away from the workpiece on the downstroke, the blade generates less friction. The blade cuts more quickly, but it enters the stock at a slight angle, increasing the risk of tearout and splintering. Hence, the greater the amount of orbital movement, the faster and rougher the results. Selecting the appropriate setting on your saw involves a compromise between speed and quality of cut.

A third type of saw is the scrolling model *(photo, left)*, which features a blade that can rotate in a complete circle within its housing, making the saw particularly well suited to intricate contour cutting. Aided by an edge guide, scrolling saws are also capable of making precise rip cuts.

Whatever type of saw you choose, one particularly desirable feature is variable speed, controlled by either trigger switch pressure or a separate dial. This added control allows you to match the cutting speed of the blade to the stock. You would generally use a higher blade speed with thicker stock.

Also look for a saw with a solid base plate that will keep the blade square to the stock for standard cuts, and one that can be tilted up to 45° for bevel cuts. The tool should include a roller guide that supports the back of the blade as it cuts. Some models also feature a sawdust blower to keep the cutting line from becoming obscured, and on-tool storage of the blade-changing and base plate adjustment wrench.

For fine cutting with reduced splintering, some models include a removable plastic insert featuring a slot that fits snugly around the blade. By bearing down on the cutting line, the insert helps to eliminate tearout on the top face of the stock.

SABER SAW SAFETY TIPS

- Do not use the saw if any of its parts are loose or damaged.

- Keep saw blades sharp, clean and undamaged; do not use a blade unless it is in good condition.

- Unplug the saw before changing a blade or making any other adjustments to the tool.

- Install a blade that is appropriate for the material you are cutting.

- Wear safety glasses and a dust mask for cutting operations that generate a large volume of wood chips or sawdust.

- Always clamp stock to a work surface.

- To avoid vibration, support the workpiece as close to the cutting line as possible.

- Keep the power cord out of the saw's cutting path; do not use the tool if the cord is frayed.

- Maintain a comfortable, balanced stance when cutting; avoid over-reaching.

- Always keep the saw base plate flush against the workpiece during a cut.

- Keep your hands away from the underside of the saw when it is operating.

- Do not touch a blade immediately after using the saw; the cutting edge can become very hot.

- Make sure the blade is not in contact with the workpiece when you turn on the saw. Allow the blade to come to full speed before feeding it into the stock.

- Do not force the saw through a cut; this can snap a blade or cause it to veer off course. Allow the blade to cut at its own speed.

- Turn off the saw before backing the blade out of a cut.

- Make sure that any keys and adjusting wrenches are removed from the tool before turning it on.

- Stay alert. Do not operate the tool when you are tired.

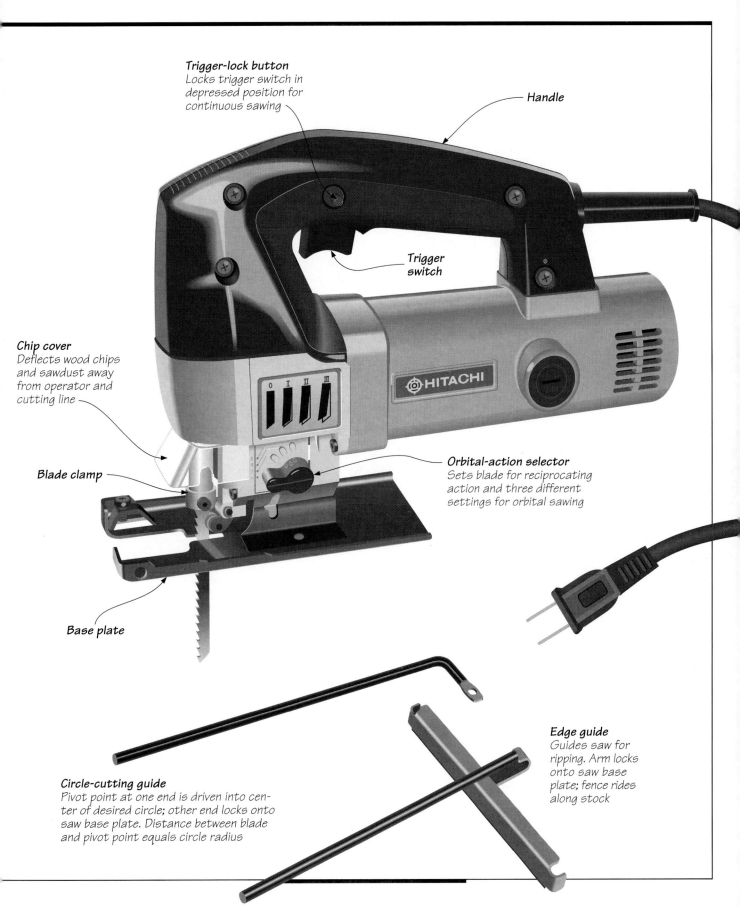

Trigger-lock button
Locks trigger switch in depressed position for continuous sawing

Handle

Trigger switch

Chip cover
Deflects wood chips and sawdust away from operator and cutting line

HITACHI

Orbital-action selector
Sets blade for reciprocating action and three different settings for orbital sawing

Blade clamp

Base plate

Edge guide
Guides saw for ripping. Arm locks onto saw base plate; fence rides along stock

Circle-cutting guide
Pivot point at one end is driven into center of desired circle; other end locks onto saw base plate. Distance between blade and pivot point equals circle radius

SABER SAW BLADES

Although the skill you bring to a project will always be reflected in the results, the single most important factor in working with a saber saw is selection of the proper blade. Most saber saws are supplied with a combination blade that works well for many cuts. But since the blades for this tool are relatively inexpensive—and because they tend to break frequently—you should keep an assortment on hand in anticipation of a variety of materials and situations. The illustration below provides a sampling of the blades that are available for the saber saw.

When buying a blade, pay particular attention to its composition, the number of teeth, the length and width of the blade, and the method of mounting. Most blades are available in high-speed steel, but bimetal types—with high-speed steel teeth welded onto a flexible body—are more durable.

Blades with a larger number of teeth per inch *(TPI)* are designed for fine cutting and tend to create a relatively narrow kerf, and produce less tearout; they also cut more slowly than models with fewer TPI. Length varies from 1¾ to 12 inches, but the standard size is 3 to 4 inches long. Not all saws accept every blade length, so consult your owner's manual for the range of sizes appropriate for your tool.

Until recently, all saber saw blades were manufactured with a universal shank—meaning that they were all mounted in the same way. In an effort to extend blade longevity, tang and hook mountings were developed *(inset, below)*. Although some models will accept the shank of any blade, others will not. Before buying blades, check the manual for the shank types suitable for your saber saw.

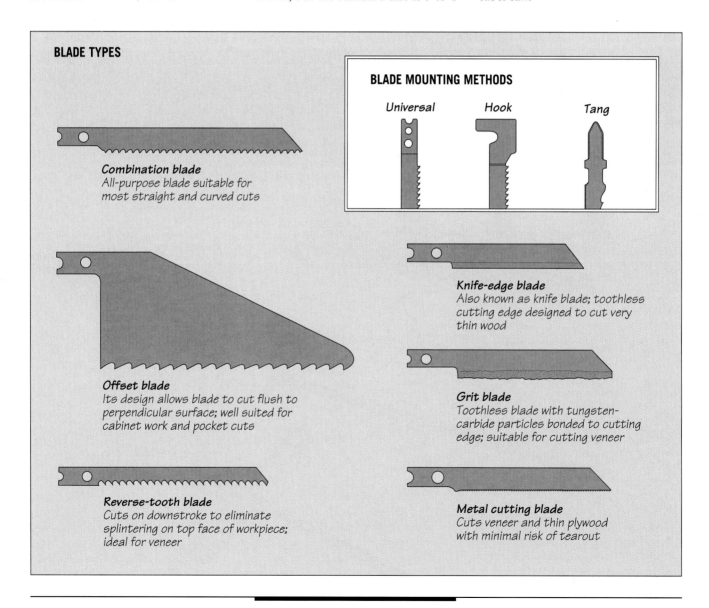

BLADE TYPES

BLADE MOUNTING METHODS

Universal   *Hook*   *Tang*

Combination blade
All-purpose blade suitable for most straight and curved cuts

Offset blade
Its design allows blade to cut flush to perpendicular surface; well suited for cabinet work and pocket cuts

Reverse-tooth blade
Cuts on downstroke to eliminate splintering on top face of workpiece; ideal for veneer

Knife-edge blade
Also known as knife blade; toothless cutting edge designed to cut very thin wood

Grit blade
Toothless blade with tungsten-carbide particles bonded to cutting edge; suitable for cutting veneer

Metal cutting blade
Cuts veneer and thin plywood with minimal risk of tearout

CHANGING A BLADE

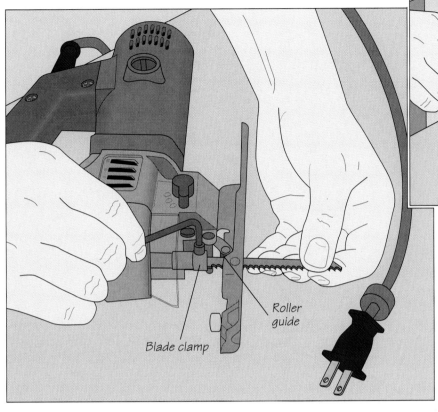

Roller
guide

Blade clamp

Installing and squaring the blade

Unplug the saw, then set it on a work surface. For the model shown, removing the blade involves loosening the clamp setscrew with the hex wrench supplied with the saw and pulling out the old blade. (On some models, the wrench is attached to the power cord.) Insert the new cutting edge in the clamp with its teeth facing the front of the saw and its back seated against the roller guide. Tighten the setscrew *(left)*. Use a try square to ascertain whether the blade is square with the base plate. If not, loosen the base plate setscrew with a hex wrench and swivel the plate until the blade butts flush against the square. Tighten the setscrew *(inset)*.

SHOP TIP

Extending blade life

If most of the stock you cut is $3/4$ inch or thinner, the top third of your blade will be the only portion showing wear. To make better use of the full length of the cutting edge, install an auxiliary shoe on the base plate of the saw once the top third of a blade begins to dull. To make the shoe, cut a piece of $1/2$-inch plywood the same length as the base plate and slightly wider. Hold the wood against the plate and mark the outline of the notch cut out for the blade. Saw out the notch and screw the auxiliary shoe in place, making sure that the back of the blade is flush against the back of the notch. (If the blade is not supported, it may wander and break when you use the saw.)

STRAIGHT CUTS

With a firm hand, a slow, steady feed rate, and a straight cutting line on your workpiece, you can make an accurate crosscut and rips using a saber saw freehand. Part of the attraction of this tool, after all, is that it cuts quickly and with a minimum of setup time.

For added precision, you can make use of an edge guide with your tool. Most saw base plates have holes machined in them to accept the arm of such a guide. The fence of the device is set for the appropriate cutting width, then the arm is fixed in place. However, the length of most commercial guides is limited, making them impractical for virtually any crosscut and for rip cuts in wide stock. As shown at right and on page 39, you can also guide the saw with a straight edge, such as a board or a try square.

For best results when making straight cuts, install a wide blade, especially if you are sawing through thick stock. Make sure the blade is long enough to cut through the wood in one pass.

Resist the temptation to hold the stock with your free hand as you are cutting. Take the an extra moment to clamp down the workpiece to a work surface, avoiding the risk of a spoiled cut or an accident.

CROSSCUTTING

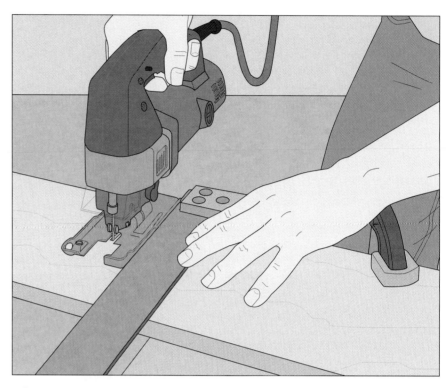

Using a try square as a guide
Clamp the stock to a work surface, arranging the board so that the cutting line is beyond the edge of the table. Align the blade with the cutting mark, then butt one edge of a try square against the saw's base plate. Make sure that the handle of the square is flush against the edge of the stock. With the saw blade clear of the stock, squeeze the trigger. Feed the cutting edge steadily into the workpiece (*above*).

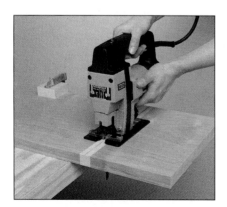

A piece of masking tape applied along the cutting line will reduce splintering while you are ripping or crosscutting.

SHOP TIP

Reducing splintering
To reduce tearout, you can either saw stock with its good face down, score the cutting line with a utility knife or cover the cutting line with a strip of tape. One other option is to install an anti-tearout jig on the underside of the base plate. The jig is similar to the auxiliary shoe shown on page 37, but the notch for the blade is only as wide as the kerf of the blade you are using. The pressure the jig exerts on the stock will keep splintering to a minimum.

RIPPING

Using a commercial edge guide

Clamp down the workpiece, making sure that your cutting line is beyond the edge of the work surface. Install a commercial edge guide on the saw, then align the blade with the mark on the board. Butt the guide against the edge of the work-piece, then lock it in place. Holding the saw firmly, feed the blade into the board, making sure that the fence stays flush against the edge of the stock.

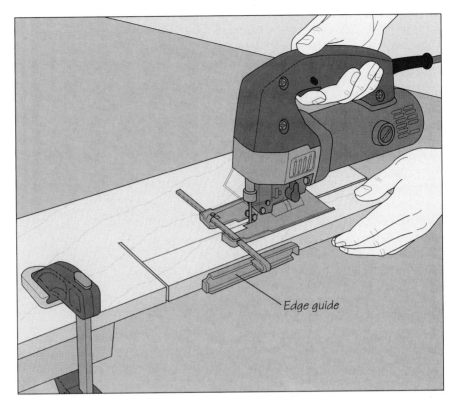

Edge guide

Using a shop-made edge guide

If you are ripping a board too wide for a commercial edge guide, use a straight-edged board to keep the blade in line *(below)*. The guide can be secured with the same clamps that hold the stock to the work surface.

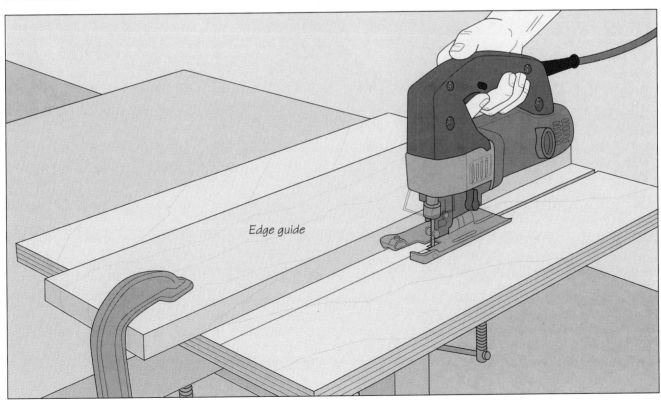

Edge guide

ANGLE CUTS

The base plate on most saber saws can be tilted to either side up to an angle of 45°, enabling the tool to make both bevel and compound cuts. Some models include a gauge that indicates the bevel angle, but you should always make a test cut to confirm that the saw is set for the angle you need.

Because the saw blade will be in contact with more of the wood surface, use a slower feed rate when making these angle cuts. For the same reason, it is generally a good idea to use a wider blade on the saw; a thin blade will be more prone to getting twisted. Although any angle cut can be made freehand, you will get better results if you take the time to set up an edge guide.

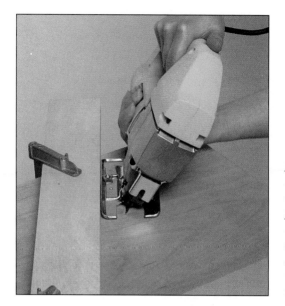

The saber saw is capable of making compound cuts—sawing through a board with the blade presented at angles other than 90° relative to both the face and edge of the stock. Two setup procedures are required: The base plate has to be tilted to the appropriate bevel angle, and an edge guide has to be clamped to the workpiece to establish the miter angle you need.

GUIDING CUTS ON THE DIAGONAL

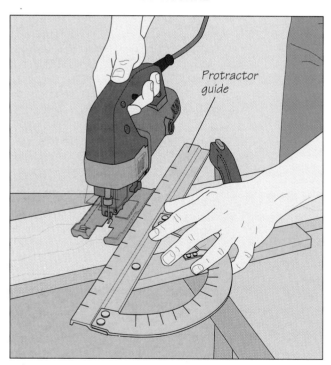

Making a miter cut with a protractor guide
Clamp the workpiece to a work surface, making certain that the cutting line is clear of the table. Set a protractor guide to the angle you wish to cut, then align the saw blade with the cutting line. Place the ruled edge of the guide against the saw's base plate; butt its other arm against the edge of the workpiece. Gripping the saw and protractor firmly, make the cut.

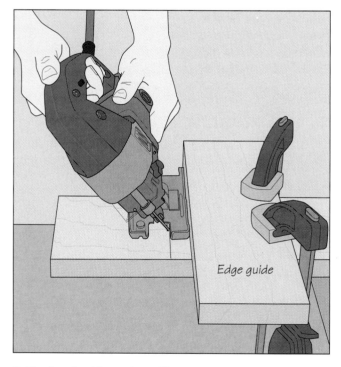

Cutting bevels with an edge guide
Loosen the setscrew on the underside of the base plate, then set the blade to the desired angle, and tighten the setscrew. The setup and cutting procedure are the same as when you are ripping lumber with a shop-made guide (*page 39*).

CURVED CUTS

The saber saw is one of the few power tools adept at cutting curves. However, you need to keep a few things in mind when you are making such cuts. Whether you are a cutting a tight curve with a scrolling model, or using a standard orbital-action or reciprocating machine to form a gentle curve, remember to feed slowly. Cutting too rapidly can bend or break the blade.

A common pitfall is blade strain. This typically occurs when the back of the blade hits the side of the kerf as it rounds a corner. The result can be a twisted or broken blade, or a blade that simply binds in the cut, marring the workpiece or forcing you to back the blade out of the kerf. The cause is invariably the use of a blade that is too wide for the curve being cut. The remedy is a narrower blade or release cuts running from the edge of the workpiece to the tightest

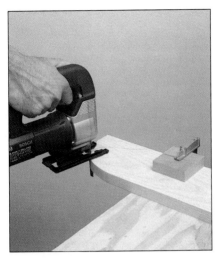

The best way to avoid binding when the edge of the workpiece is a short distance from the cutting path is to veer off the cutting line and saw to the edge of the workpiece; then come back and continue the cut at a gentler angle.

parts of the curve. Rather than the blade binding in the kerf at these points, the waste will fall away, giving the cutting edge some room to maneuver.

Like the band saw, the saber saw is useful for cutting circles. Although you can make such cuts freehand, both store-bought and shop-made jigs *(page 43)* will improve precision. In either case, make sure you secure the stock to a work surface. Depending on whether the circle or the surrounding stock will be the finished product, you can get the blade to the cutting line by making a plunge cut *(page 44)*, boring a hole *(page 45)*, or sawing a wedge out of the surrounding stock.

Before starting a cut, make sure that the cutting line is clearly marked on the workpiece. Check, too, that any clamps used to secure the stock are not in the path of the saw.

CUTTING A CURVE FREEHAND

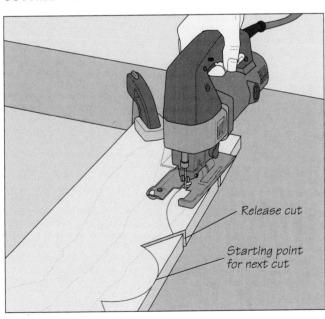
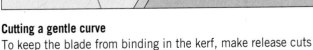

Release cut

Starting point for next cut

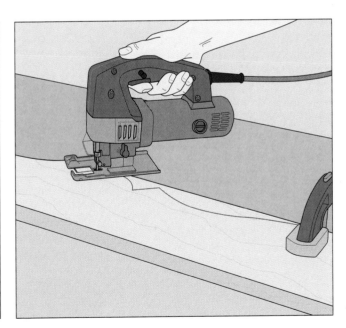

Cutting a gentle curve
To keep the blade from binding in the kerf, make release cuts from the edge of the workpiece to the tightest turns. Begin by aligning the blade with the cutting line at the end or edge of the workpiece. Feed the saw into the stock, guiding the tool slowly to keep the blade on line *(above, left)*. For a cut like the one shown here, saw to the first release cut; once the waste falls away, turn off the saw. Resume at the next point where the cutting mark contacts the edge of the stock and work between release cuts *(above, right)*. Complete the job by sawing back from the opposite end of the line to the final release cut.

SHOP TIP

Making release and tangent cuts
Depending on the curve you are cutting, you may need to "straighten out" the saber saw blade during the cut. Otherwise, you risk binding the blade in the kerf. For a curve that will leave a concave arc in a workpiece (right, above), make a series of straight release cuts from the end of the stock to the cutting line. As the blade rounds the contours and reaches the release cuts, waste pieces will fall away, giving the blade room to turn. For a convex arc (right, below), begin at one end of the cutting line, but as soon as the blade begins to bind, veer off to the edge or end of the stock. Then return to the cutting line, continuing in this fashion until the cut is completed.

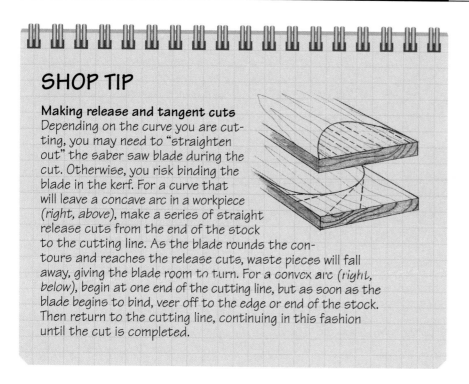

FREEHAND ARTISTRY WITH A SCROLLING SAW

Following an intricate path
If the operation starts with a straight cut, feed the saw into the stock as you would a standard crosscut or rip cut. As the blade reaches the curved portion of the cutting line, release the scroller lock button, then use the scrolling knob to steer the cutting edge in the desired direction (see photo page 34). Continue to the end of the cutting line, gripping the saw firmly with one hand and guiding it with your other hand on the scrolling knob. On the model shown, the blade can also be steered along a curved path by exerting moderate steering pressure on the handle.

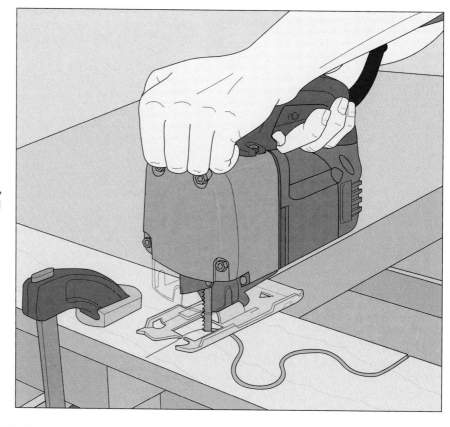

CIRCLE CUTTING

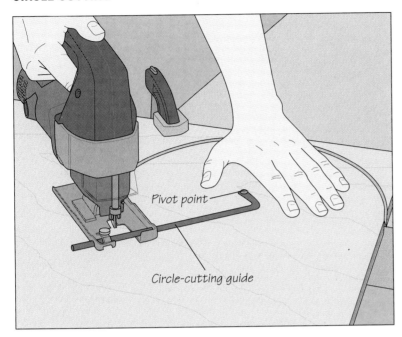

Pivot point

Circle-cutting guide

Using a commercial circle-cutting guide

Clamp down the stock with as much of the workpiece as possible extending off the table. Make sure the setup is steady, however. If the area inside the circle will be the waste wood, make a plunge cut *(page 44)* or bore a hole *(page 45)* within the cutting line; if the material surrounding the circle will be the waste, make a release cut to the cutting line from the edge of the stock. Fit a commercial circle-cutting guide on the arm of the saw and drive the pivot point into the stock at the center of the circle you will be cutting. Adjust the guide until the distance between the blade and the pivot point equals the radius of the circle. Holding the saw and the stock firmly, cut out the circle *(left)*. To avoid sawing into the work surface, turn off the saw and reposition the workpiece as necessary.

BUILD IT YOURSELF

CIRCLE-CUTTING JIG

To cut circles that exceed the capacity of a commercial guide, use a shop-made jig customized for your saber saw. The exact size of the jig can vary, but the dimensions in the illustration at right will yield a jig large enough to cut a circle to the edges of a 4-by-8 panel.

To make the jig, remove the blade from your saw and outline its base plate on a piece of ½-inch plywood. Reinstall the blade and cut along the marks, making the section that will be beneath the base plate slightly larger than the plate. Streamline the jig by trimming it down to the shape of an L, then cut out the notch for the blade. Screw the jig to the base plate, ensuring that the back of the blade is flush against the bottom of the notch. Next, use a pencil to mark a pivot line on the jig that is aligned with the blade.

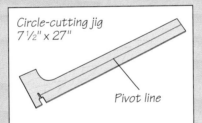

Circle-cutting jig
7 ½" x 27"

Pivot line

Cut into the stock to bring the blade up to the outline of the circle you will be cutting. Then drive a nail or a screw into the jig on the pivot line at the center of the circle. Cut the circle as you would when using a commercial guide.

Pivot point

PLUNGE CUTTING

The saber saw's design makes it ideal for the tricky job of making interior cuts. There are two ways to begin the operation. You can use a drill to bore a hole *(page 45)* or plunge the blade into the workpiece, as shown below.

This second method will make the cut much more quickly, but it is also a little more challenging to perform. It takes some practice to keep the blade from skating on the surface of the stock. For best results, work with a short, stiff blade in the saw.

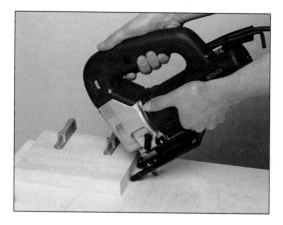

Make sure you have a firm grip on your saber saw when making a plunge cut, otherwise the blade will tend to jump off the surface of the wood at the start of the cut.

MAKING AN INTERIOR CUT

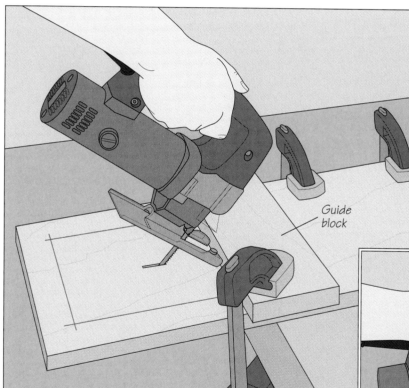

Guide block

2 Completing the cut
Remove the guide block and continue the cut. To remove the bulk of the waste in a single pass, saw to one of the cutting lines. For the rectangular outline shown, follow the marks, but do not try to cut the corners square. Instead, bypass the corners with contour cuts *(below)*, continuing until you reach your starting point and the waste piece falls away.

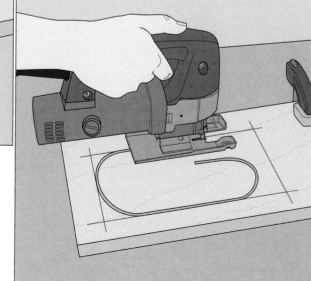

1 Plunging into the stock
Align a guide block with one of the cutting lines and clamp it in place as shown. Resting the front of the base plate on the workpiece flush against the guide block, pivot the saw forward until the blade is above the stock. Then, gripping the saw firmly, turn it on and slowly lower the blade into the stock *(above)*, keeping the base plate butted against the guide block. Once the saw sits flat on the workpiece, turn off the tool.

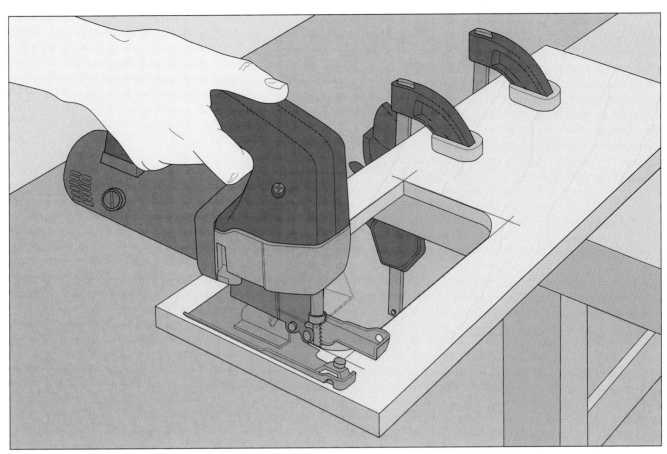

3 **Squaring the corners**
Cut away the remaining waste with two intersecting cuts at each corner. Holding the edge of the blade flat against one of the cut edges, saw along the line until the blade reaches the corner *(above)*. Repeat this procedure on the adjoining side to clear the waste wood from the first corner. Then do the same thing at the remaining corners.

SHOP TIP

Boring access holes
An alternative to making a plunge cut in a workpiece is to bore a hole in which you can insert the blade. Install a brad-point bit on a drill press or electric drill; the bit diameter should be wider than the width of the blade. At each corner bore a hole that just touches the cutting lines on both sides. The saw blade can then be inserted in the hole to cut to the adjoining corner.

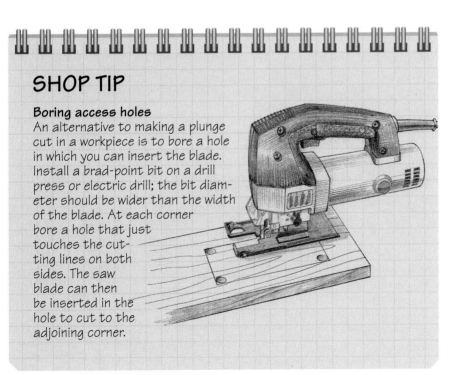

CUTTING DUPLICATE PIECES

The saber saw lends itself to the production of multiple copies of a shape. Provided the stock is not too thick, stack sawing is an effective method for cutting duplicate pieces. Using this approach, layers of stock are fastened together and the pieces are cut in a single operation. Not only is stack sawing more efficient than cutting all the pieces separately, it ensures that the finished products are exact copies.

Some woodworkers use nails or screws to bond the layers together in preparation for cutting; others prefer clamps. Both approaches can be hazardous, however, if the blade accidentally strikes a fastener or clamp. A safer way is to use double-sided tape to hold the pieces together.

There are some limitations on stack sawing with a saber saw. First, the blade must be longer than the combined thicknesses of the workpieces. Depending on the model you have, you can buy saber saw blades up to 12 inches long, but do not attempt to use a blade that is too short. You will also probably need to make the cut fairly slowly.

Another option for repeat curved cuts is to use the first piece you cut as an edge guide for subsequent cuts. Clamping the guide to the workpieces can make a contour cut as straightforward as a crosscut.

STACK SAWING

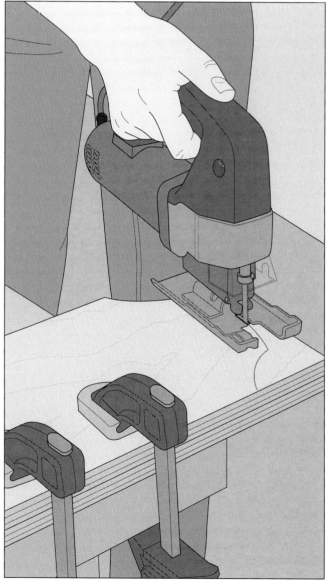

Cutting through stacked wood
Use double-sided tape to fasten the layers of stock together *(above, left)*, making sure that the ends and edges of the pieces are perfectly aligned. Mark a cutting line on the top piece, then clamp the stack to a work surface with the portion to be cut completely off the table. Align the saw blade with the line, then make the cut as you would for any other curve *(above, right)*.

REPEAT CURVED CUTS

1 Setting up an edge guide

To cut a relatively gentle curve in several workpieces, saw the first piece freehand, then use it as an edge guide in making the others. Cut the guide slightly longer than the subsequent pieces to help in aligning the saw. Since the tool's base plate will be riding along the guide, carefully sand the curved edge. Set the next piece of stock on a work surface. Mark a cutting line on its leading edge. Then align the blade with the mark and butt the edge guide flush against the saw's base plate. Measure the gap between the back edges of the two pieces at both ends to make sure they are perfectly parallel, then clamp the guide in place as shown.

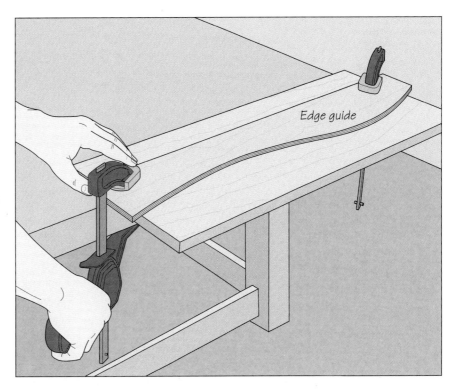

Edge guide

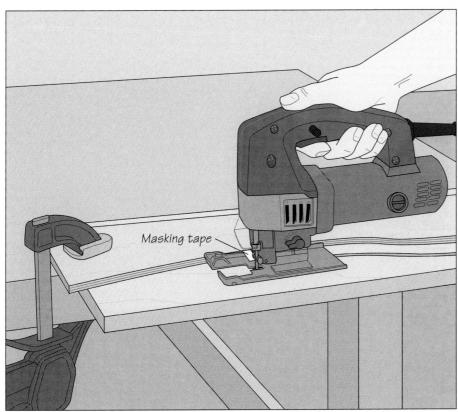

Masking tape

2 Making the cut

To help in keeping the saw directly on its cutting path, place a small strip of masking tape on the base plate in line with the blade. To start the cut, butt the base plate up against the edge guide and align the blade with the cutting mark. Feed the blade into the stock, keeping the part of the base plate with the masking tape flush against the edge guide (left).

ELECTRIC DRILL

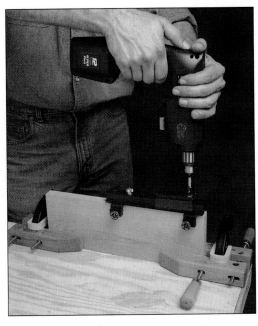

Coupled with a commercial doweling jig, this cordless drill can bore holes for dowels at any interval. The depth collar on the bit controls the drilling depth precisely.

Despite the fact that it is capable of one basic action—rotating whatever is clutched in its jaws—the electric drill is probably the most frequently used portable power tool in a woodworker's shop. The better-quality models are suited for more than simply boring holes; they are true multipurpose tools.

You can rely on your drill to make precise holes, ranging in size from tiny $\frac{1}{32}$-inch incisions to 4-inch cavities cut with a hole saw. With a stop collar or shop-made depth guide fastened to the bit, you have the ability to precisely control the depth of the hole you are making. Certain specialized bits for the power drill let you control the shape of the hole as well. A counterbore bit, for example, makes three sizes of holes in a single operation: one as a pilot hole for a screw tip, a slightly larger opening for the screw shank, and a hole large enough for a wood plug to conceal the head of the screw.

Other accessories greatly expand the portable drill's capabilities. Depending on the attachment, a drill can drive screws and nails; shape, sand and scrape wood surfaces; and power a grinding wheel for sharpening bits. Attached to a guide, the tool gains enough stability to cut wood plugs, a task that would be difficult to perform well with a hand-held drill. Mounted in a stand, the drill becomes a stationary tool, freeing your hands to manipulate the workpiece. A stand will also give your drill a level of precision approaching that of a drill press.

Portable drills are classified according to the maximum bit shank diameter that can be fitted into their chucks. The most common home workshop sizes are $\frac{1}{4}$-, $\frac{3}{8}$-, and $\frac{1}{2}$-inch drills. A system of gears between a drill's chuck and motor rotates the chuck at a certain speed and with a certain amount of torque, or twisting force. Depending on the job at hand, either drill speed or torque will be the crucial factor. Higher speeds are needed for small-diameter holes and for jobs like sanding or scraping; higher torque will help out when you are making larger holes.

In general, the higher a drill's maximum speed, the less torque it can generate. A typical $\frac{1}{4}$-inch drill rated at 3 amps can produce speeds up to 4000 rpm, but it will lack the necessary power for boring larger holes in hardwood. A $\frac{1}{2}$-inch hammer drill rated at 4.5 amps develops enough torque to punch a hole in concrete, but the tool will not run faster than 850 rpm, insufficient to spin a sanding disk rapidly enough for smoothing wood. Between the two extremes is the $\frac{3}{8}$-inch drill. With typical speeds as high as 1200 rpm and ample torque, it is considered the best all-purpose drill for most woodworkers.

A $\frac{1}{4}$-inch brad-point bit bores a series of overlapping holes for a mortise in a cabriole leg. After a chisel has squared the mortise corners, the leg will be ready to accept a rail tenon.

ANATOMY OF AN ELECTRIC DRILL

Although all electric drills operate in essentially the same way, woodworkers often keep several different models on hand to take care of any drilling operation. For most applications, a corded ⅜-inch variable speed, reversible drill, such as the model illustrated on page 51, is the best choice. A ¼-inch drill also has its special uses. Although it lacks the power and bit capacity of a larger drill, a ¼-inch model can generate more rpm, enabling it to bore cleaner small diameter holes.

A third choice of many woodworkers is the cordless drill. Early models often sacrificed power for portability, but more recent versions have solved this problem and can produce enough torque for most drilling jobs. A common feature is an adjustable slip-clutch mechanism, designed to make driving and removing screws easy and precise. The clutch allows the bit to spin only as fast as the screw turns; when the screw stops rotating so too does the bit. This prevents the bit from stripping the screw head or slipping off the screw and possibly marring the workpiece. For maximum flexibility, many cordless drills offer a range of slip-clutch settings.

Whatever the type or size of a drill, there are several other features you should keep in mind. A reversing switch is essential for removing screws; it can also be useful for withdrawing a bit that is stuck in a hole. A chuck key that can be stored on the drill or the power cord is a small but significant convenience. For prolonged operations such as sanding or scraping, make sure your drill has a locking switch that will keep the motor running without requiring that the trigger switch be depressed.

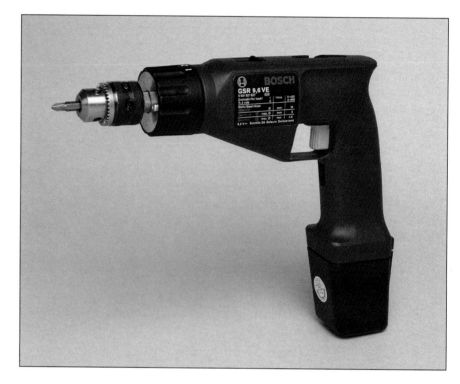

This cordless drill/driver takes the portability of the electric drill one step further. Powered by rechargeable nickel-cadmium batteries, the tool can be taken anywhere in the shop.

ELECTRIC DRILL SAFETY TIPS

• Always wear safety glasses when operating a drill; also put on a dust mask if you are using a sanding or scraping accessory.

• Do not use the drill if any of its parts is loose or damaged; inspect your drill bits and accessories before drilling.

• Keep all cords clear of the cutting area.

• Disconnect the drill from its power source before changing a bit or accessory, or making any other adjustments to the tool.

• Keep your hands away from the underside of a workpiece when the bit is cutting into it.

• When installing a bit, make sure you insert it fully into the chuck.

• Do not tighten the chuck by hand; insert the chuck key in each of the three holes in the chuck to tighten.

• Remove the chuck key after installing a bit or accessory.

• Keep the drill's air vents clear of sawdust to avoid overheating the motor.

• Avoid steadying a workpiece by hand; clamp your stock to a work surface whenever possible to keep both your hands free to operate the tool.

• Maintain a comfortable, balanced stance when operating the drill; avoid over-reaching.

• Do not force the drill; allow it to bore at its own speed, withdrawing the bit from the hole periodically to clear out the waste, if necessary.

• Do not wear loose-fitting clothing or jewelry. They can be caught by a spinning bit.

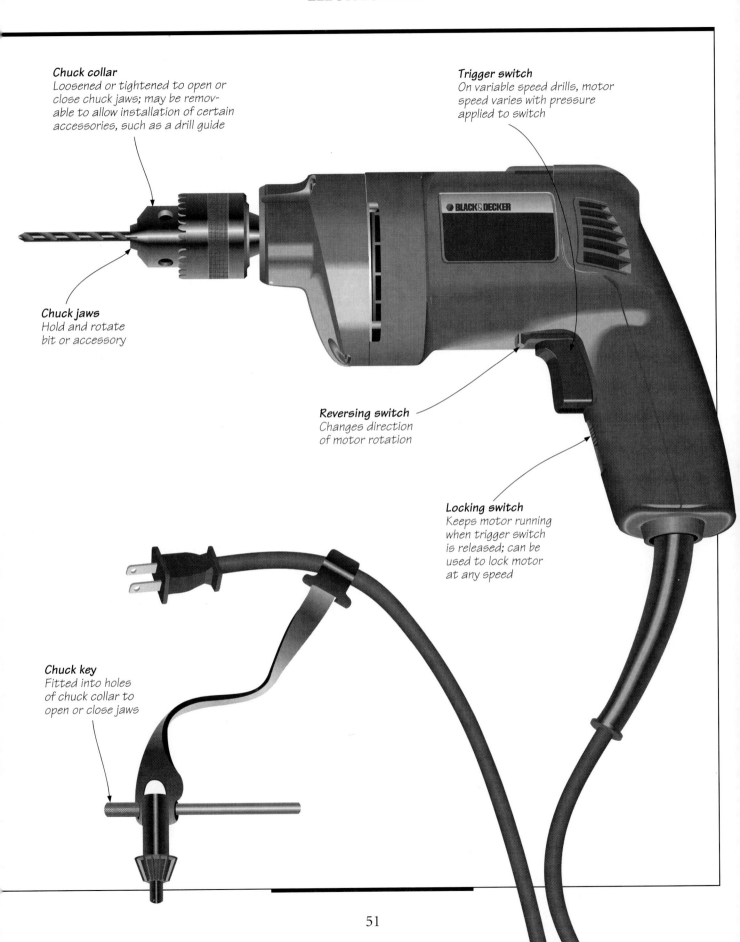

Chuck collar
Loosened or tightened to open or close chuck jaws; may be removable to allow installation of certain accessories, such as a drill guide

Trigger switch
On variable speed drills, motor speed varies with pressure applied to switch

Chuck jaws
Hold and rotate bit or accessory

Reversing switch
Changes direction of motor rotation

Locking switch
Keeps motor running when trigger switch is released; can be used to lock motor at any speed

Chuck key
Fitted into holes of chuck collar to open or close jaws

BLACK&DECKER

DRILL BITS AND ACCESSORIES

Your electric drill's versatility is limited only by the range of bits and accessories you accumulate in the shop. With the appropriate attachment in its chuck, the drill can be an ideal tool for a great many jobs, making it invaluable at many stages of a project. A flap sander and a stand, for example, transform the drill into a stationary tool for smoothing wood. With a rotary rasp, the tool can shape decorative contours. A right-angle head or a flexible shaft will get a bit into tight spots. Once the job is done, a bit sharpener will restore sharp cutting edges to ensure that you bore cleanly drilled holes.

Nevertheless, bits are likely to be the accessories you use most. As shown below, a wide array of these implements is available, from twist and brad-point bits for boring holes of different diameters and depths to counterbore bits for drilling recessed screw holes.

The popular twist bit bores holes from 1/32 to 1/2 inch in diameter. Originally designed for drilling into metal, twist bits have a tendency to skate on a surface before penetrating it. You can improve their performance by punching a starting hole in your workpiece with an awl before boring a hole.

Most woodworkers prefer brad-point bits. Available with either carbon steel, high-speed steel or carbide-tipped cutting edges, the sharpened centerpoint of a brad-point bit allows accurate positioning. Better-quality bits feature two spurs on the perimeter that score the circumference of the hole before the chipping bevels clear away the stock. Twist bits, however, are a better choice for angled holes.

Although drill bits are virtually maintenance-free, remember that they will only work properly for as long as they are kept sharp.

A RANGE OF BITS

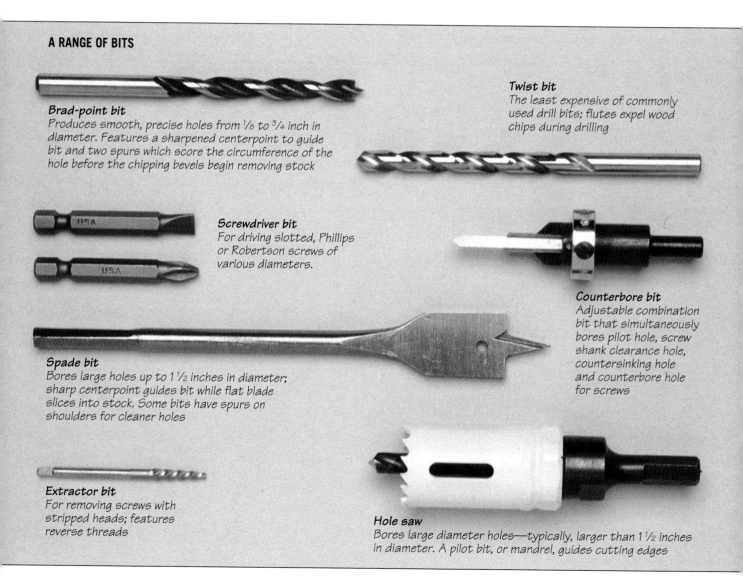

Brad-point bit
Produces smooth, precise holes from 1/8 to 3/4 inch in diameter. Features a sharpened centerpoint to guide bit and two spurs which score the circumference of the hole before the chipping bevels begin removing stock

Twist bit
The least expensive of commonly used drill bits; flutes expel wood chips during drilling

Screwdriver bit
For driving slotted, Phillips or Robertson screws of various diameters.

Counterbore bit
Adjustable combination bit that simultaneously bores pilot hole, screw shank clearance hole, countersinking hole and counterbore hole for screws

Spade bit
Bores large holes up to 1 1/2 inches in diameter; sharp centerpoint guides bit while flat blade slices into stock. Some bits have spurs on shoulders for cleaner holes

Extractor bit
For removing screws with stripped heads; features reverse threads

Hole saw
Bores large diameter holes—typically, larger than 1 1/2 inches in diameter. A pilot bit, or mandrel, guides cutting edges

A SAMPLE OF ACCESSORIES

Plug cutter
Cuts wood plugs up to ½ inch long to conceal counterbored screws; chamfers one end of plug for easy installation

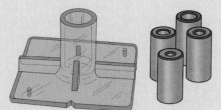

Drill guide
For keeping drill at fixed angle to flat or round stock. Bushings accommodate various bit diameters.

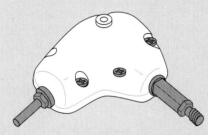

Stop collar
Also called drill stop or depth gauge; for drilling to an exact depth. Available in sets matching bit diameters, typically from ⅛ to ½ inch. Hex wrench supplied for installing on bit

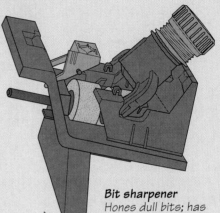

Right-angle head
For working in tight corners; allows accessory in chuck to operate at 90° angle to body of drill. Installed between chuck and drill body

Bit sharpener
Hones dull bits; has grinding wheels and chuck to hold bits

Nail spinner
Drives finishing nails from 1 to 3 inches long into hardwood without predrilled pilot hole

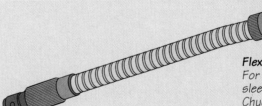

Flexible shaft
For drilling in tight areas; sleeve can bend up to 90°. Chuck accepts most bits

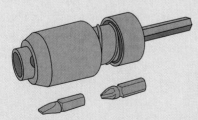

Clutch adapter
Drives screws without having to drill pilot holes; holds screw securely until head is flush with surface, then clutch disengages to avoid stripping screw head

Flap sander
For sanding curved or contoured surfaces; features aluminum head which spins sanding strips

BORING HOLES

Boring a hole into a piece of wood may seem like a simple task. But when you consider that some wood species are harder to penetrate than others, and that holes for woodworking projects sometimes need to be drilled at precise angles and to exact depths, it becomes clear that this deceptively easy operation holds the potential for error. Precision is as important in drilling as in any other phase of a project. A dowel hole that is off-center or too deep, or a pocket hole drilled at the wrong angle, can mar a project as badly as an inaccurate saw cut or a poorly applied finish.

For most operations, accuracy begins with the proper setup. While you can depend on a steady hand to bore a perfectly straight hole, there are a wide variety of commercial guides to ensure that your drill bit will not wander off-line.

A couple of simple shop-made jigs shown in this chapter make it easy to drill both straight and angled holes.

If you are using a twist bit, punch a starting hole for the bit with an awl. To prevent splintering as the bit exits from a workpiece, clamp a support board between the stock and the work surface. For best results, avoid starting a hole with the drill running at full speed. Instead, begin slowly, then gradually increase the speed as you drill. Control the depth of a hole by installing a commercial stop collar on the bit or using the shop-made alternative.

A commercial guide steadies a drill for a precise angled hole. This model can also hold the drill perfectly perpendicular to a surface.

STRAIGHT AND ANGLED HOLES

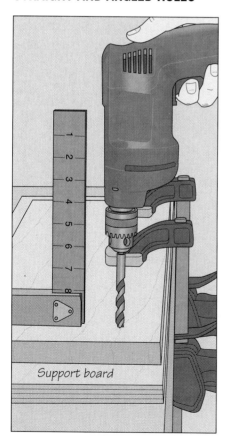

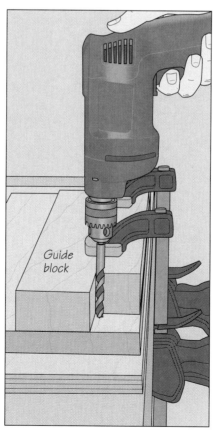

Boring a straight hole
A try square or a shop-made block will help you keep a drill bit perpendicular to a workpiece when you bore a hole. To use the square, line up its handle with the mark for the hole, with the blade pointing up. Centering the bit over the mark, align it with the blade and bore the hole *(far left)*. Be sure to keep the bit parallel to the square throughout the operation. To make the guide block, cut a 90° angle wedge out of one corner of a board. Center the bit over the mark, then butt the notched corner of the guide block against it. Clamp the block in place. Keeping the bit flush against the corner of the block *(near left)*, bore the hole.

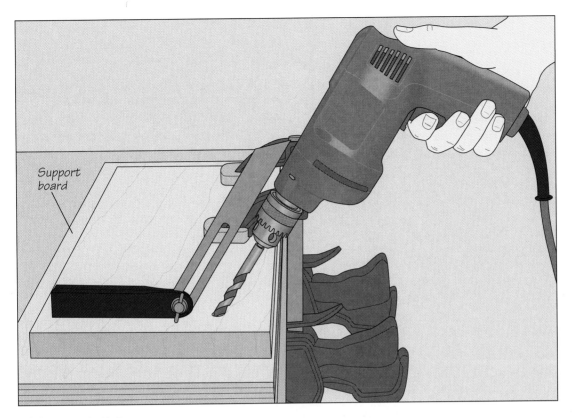

**Guiding an angled hole
with a bevel gauge**
Set a sliding bevel to the appropriate
angle, then line up its handle beside
the point where you need the hole.
Center the bit over the mark, then
bore the hole *(above)*, keeping the bit
parallel to the blade while you drill.

SHOP TIP

Guide block for angled holes
To make a guide block for drilling into
a workpiece at an angle, bore at
a 90° angle through a small wood
block with the same bit you will be
using for the angled hole. Then make
a miter cut at one end of the block
trimming the wood at the same angle
as the hole you will be drilling. Cut a
notch in one side of the block to
facilitate clamping, and make a
V-shaped notch at the bottom
to help you pinpoint the tip of
the bit. Clamp the block in
place when using it to bore
a hole.

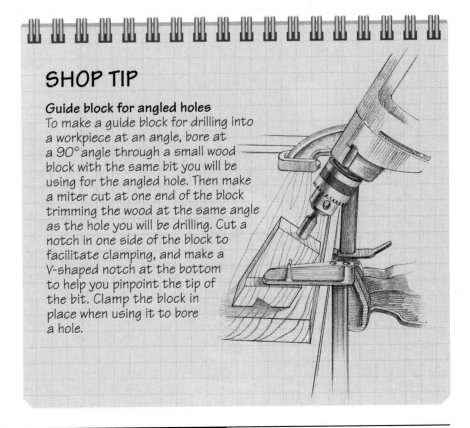

WIDE AND DEEP HOLES

Using spade bits and hole saws

Drill holes up to 1½ inches in diameter with a spade bit; for wider holes, use a hole saw. In either case, punch a starting hole in the workpiece with an awl. For the spade bit, put the centerpoint in the indentation left by the awl. Holding the tool steady as shown, bore the hole *(near right)*. If you are using a hole saw, install an auxiliary handle whenever possible to give the drill more stability. In any case, center the pilot bit over the starting point, and holding the drill with both hands, start drilling slowly. Increase the speed gradually, feeding with only enough pressure to keep the bit cutting into the wood *(far right)*.

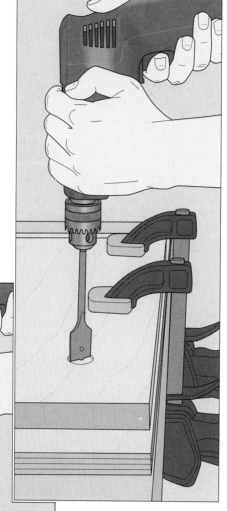

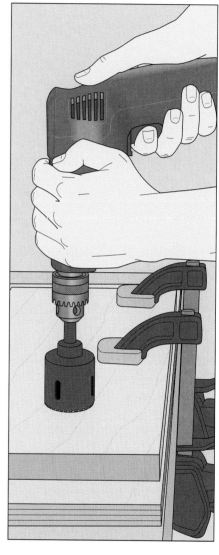

First hole

Boring a deep hole

To bore a hole that is deeper than your bit is long, make intersecting holes from opposite ends of the workpiece. Begin by punching starting holes at the same point on both ends of the stock. Then secure the workpiece in a handscrew and clamp it to a work surface with one of the starting points facing up. Centering the bit over the mark, bore a hole slightly more than halfway through the stock. Flip the workpiece over and clamp it in position. Center the bit over the other starting point and complete the drilling operation *(left)*.

Widening a hole

To widen a hole that has already been bored by a brad-point or a spade bit, you will need a solid surface to brace the centerpoint of the bit against. First plug the hole by tapping a dowel into it. Use a dowel the same diameter as the hole for a snug fit and make sure that it is flush with the surface of the workpiece. Mark the center of the dowel, then install the appropriate bit in the drill and bore the wider hole *(inset)*.

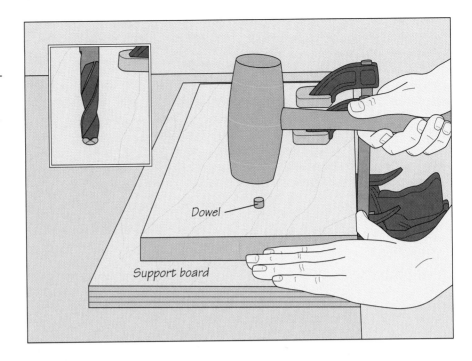

Dowel

Support board

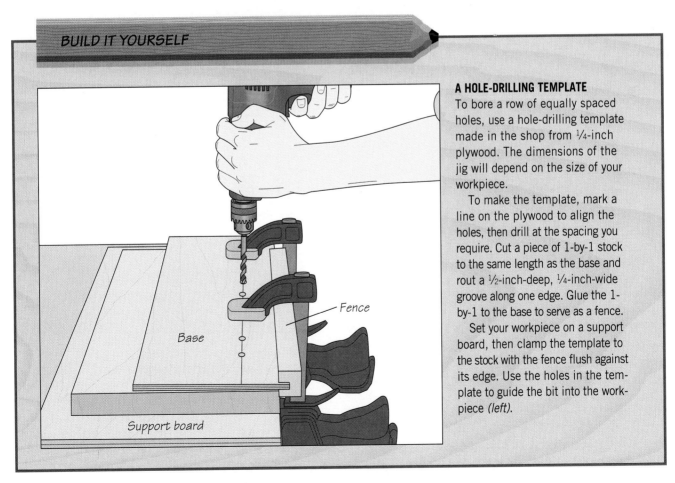

BUILD IT YOURSELF

Base

Fence

Support board

A HOLE-DRILLING TEMPLATE

To bore a row of equally spaced holes, use a hole-drilling template made in the shop from ¼-inch plywood. The dimensions of the jig will depend on the size of your workpiece.

To make the template, mark a line on the plywood to align the holes, then drill at the spacing you require. Cut a piece of 1-by-1 stock to the same length as the base and rout a ½-inch-deep, ¼-inch-wide groove along one edge. Glue the 1-by-1 to the base to serve as a fence.

Set your workpiece on a support board, then clamp the template to the stock with the fence flush against its edge. Use the holes in the template to guide the bit into the workpiece *(left)*.

SCREW HOLES AND PLUGS

Driving a screw into hardwood without predrilling the hole risks splitting the workpiece or breaking off the head of the screw. Depending on how deeply you need to sink the screw, you may have to bore up to four overlapping holes of different diameters, one inside the next. If you want the screw head to sit on the surface of the wood, bore a pilot hole for the threads and a clearance hole for the shank. For the best grip, a pilot hole should be slightly smaller than the threads of the screw. To set the head flush with

the surface, bore a countersinking hole. If you wish to conceal the screw under a wood plug, add a counterbore hole.

There are two ways to bore holes for screws. You can use a different bit for each hole or, as shown below, bore them simultaneously with a counterbore bit.

Thanks to their variable speed and reversible motors, electric drills are ideal for driving or removing screws rapidly with a minimum of effort.

DRIVING SCREWS

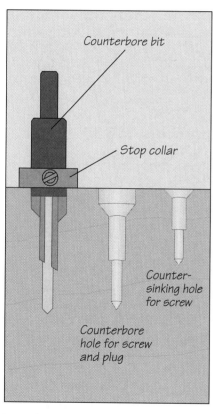

Counterbore bit

Stop collar

Counter-
sinking hole
for screw

Counterbore
hole for screw
and plug

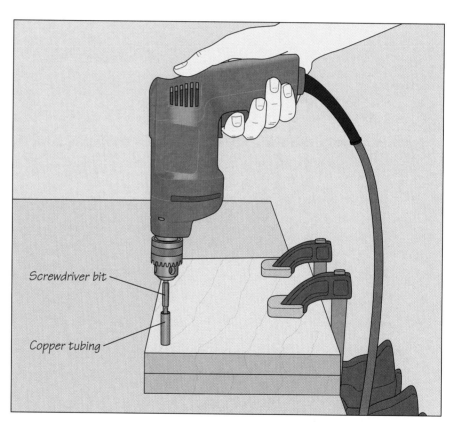

Screwdriver bit

Copper tubing

Preparing screw holes

To screw two pieces of stock together, fit your drill with a counterbore bit of a size appropriate to the size of your hardware. Such a bit will bore a pilot hole and has a stop collar that slides up and down to adjust it for making either counterbore or countersinking holes *(above, left)*. Clamp the workpieces one atop the other on a work surface, then bore the hole. If you will be using a screwdriver to install the screw, coat the threads with candle wax to make the fastener easier to drive. To use the drill, install a screwdriver bit and set the screw in the hole by hand. For a slotted head screw, slip a short length of copper tubing around it to prevent the bit from slipping off the head and marring the stock. Fit the bit into the screw head and apply light pressure as you slowly start the drill; gradually increase the feed pressure and drill speed as the screw takes hold.

CUTTING WOOD PLUGS

Using a plug cutter

Fit your drill into a commercial guide following the manufacturer's instructions. On the model shown, you must remove the chuck from the drill, attach the center spindle of the guide to the tool, then replace the chuck on the spindle. Next, install a plug cutter in the chuck and slip the spindle onto the guide rods. Adjust the cutting depth with the locking collar. Keeping the guide steady on the workpiece, raise the tool to hold the cutter just above the stock. Turn on the power and push the drill down to feed the cutter into the wood. Release the pressure when the center spindle hits the locking collar. Free the plug from the stock with a chisel.

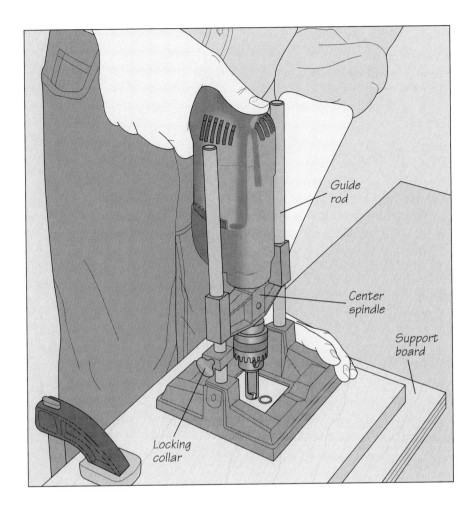

Guide rod

Center spindle

Support board

Locking collar

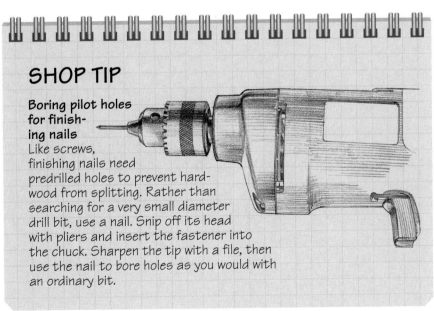

SHOP TIP

Boring pilot holes for finishing nails
Like screws, finishing nails need predrilled holes to prevent hardwood from splitting. Rather than searching for a very small diameter drill bit, use a nail. Snip off its head with pliers and insert the fastener into the chuck. Sharpen the tip with a file, then use the nail to bore holes as you would with an ordinary bit.

PORTABLE DRILL JOINERY

Mortise-and-tenon joint

Dowel joint

The portable electric drill may not be the first tool that springs to mind when you think of joinery. Only the most innovative woodworker would contemplate using the tool to make a dovetail or finger joint, for example. Nevertheless, for any method of joinery requiring a cavity cut to an exact depth, the drill is a workable choice. It is especially practical for mortise-and-tenon and dowel joints.

For the mortise-and-tenon, the tool will rough out a mortise, although you will need to square the corners with a chisel. A stop collar or a depth guide *(page 61)* will guarantee that the bottom of the cavity will be even and level.

A brad-point bit will produce the best results. Choose one with a diameter equal to the width of the mortise outline, rather than relying on overlapping cuts with a smaller bit. Most woodworkers prefer to cut the tenon first and then use it to mark the dimensions of the mortise.

A drill can perform all the steps needed to prepare stock for a dowel joint. The key to an accurate joint is to center the dowel holes on the workpiece; otherwise, the two pieces being joined will be out of alignment. Center your bit on the edge of a workpiece with a commercial doweling jig or build your own center-drilling device *(page 63)*.

MAKING A MORTISE

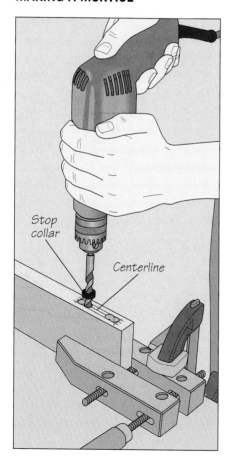

Stop collar

Centerline

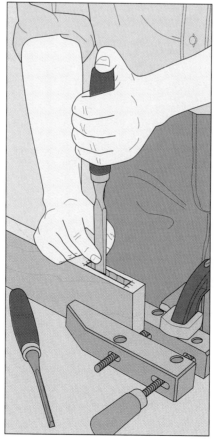

Cutting the mortise

Clamp the workpiece in handscrews, then secure the stock to a work surface as shown, with the mortise outline facing up. Mark a line through the center of the outline to help you align the bit. Install a stop collar and adjust the drilling depth to correspond to the length of the tenon. With the bit directly over the centerline, bore a hole at each end of the mortise outline; hold the drill with both hands to keep the tool perpendicular to the edge of the stock. Then make a series of overlapping holes *(far left)* to remove as much waste as possible. Square the mortise with a chisel, keeping the blade perfectly vertical and its beveled edge facing the inside of the mortise *(near left)*.

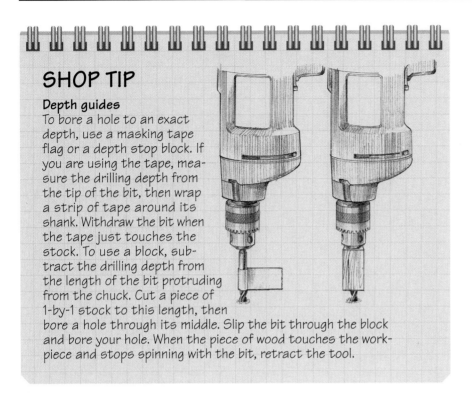

SHOP TIP

Depth guides
To bore a hole to an exact depth, use a masking tape flag or a depth stop block. If you are using the tape, measure the drilling depth from the tip of the bit, then wrap a strip of tape around its shank. Withdraw the bit when the tape just touches the stock. To use a block, subtract the drilling depth from the length of the bit protruding from the chuck. Cut a piece of 1-by-1 stock to this length, then bore a hole through its middle. Slip the bit through the block and bore your hole. When the piece of wood touches the workpiece and stops spinning with the bit, retract the tool.

DRILLING A DOWEL JOINT

1 Boring the dowel holes
Secure one of the boards to be joined with handscrews as you would when drilling a mortise *(page 60)*. Clamp a doweling jig onto the edge of the workpiece. The model shown centers the dowel holes on the stock and spaces them at the interval you choose. To avoid splitting the boards, use grooved dowels that are no more than half the thickness of the stock. Fit your drill with a bit the same diameter as the dowels, then install a stop collar to mark the drilling depth, which should be slightly more than half the length of the dowels. Slide the bushing carrier along the jig and insert the appropriate bushing in the hole through which you are planning to drill. (The bushing ensures that the bit is kept perfectly square to the board.) Holding the drill firmly, bore the hole. Make the remaining holes for the dowels.

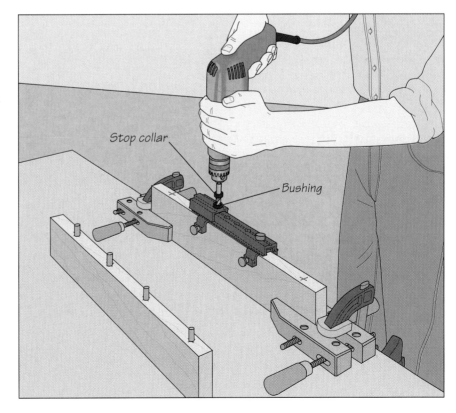

Stop collar

Bushing

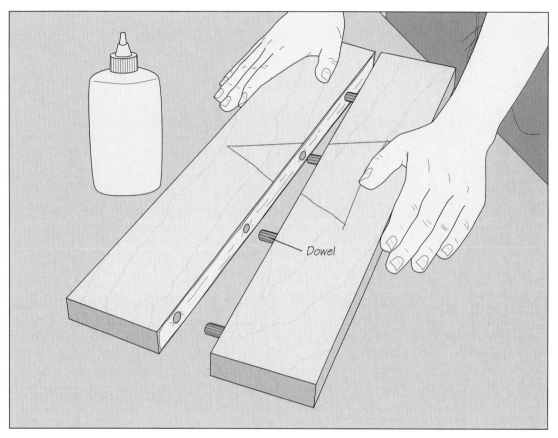

Dowel

2 Gluing up the boards

Apply a thin bead of glue and spread it evenly along the edges that will be joined. Also dab a small amount of adhesive in the bottom of each dowel hole; a pencil can be useful in getting the glue in the holes. Avoid spreading glue directly on the dowels; they absorb moisture quickly and will swell, making them difficult to fit into their holes. Insert the dowels, then tap them into final position with a mallet. Avoid pounding, which can cause a board to split. Close up the joint, then use bar clamps to hold the pieces in place until the glue is dry.

SHOP TIP

Using dowel centers
Instead of relying on a jig when boring dowel holes, you can use dowel centers to ensure that the holes are precisely centered on the boards being joined. After making the holes in one board, insert the proper-sized dowel centers. Then set the board on a flat surface alongside the board to which it will be joined. Align their ends and butt the two boards together. The pointed ends of the dowel centers will punch impressions on the stock, providing starting points for the mating dowel holes.

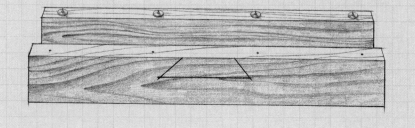

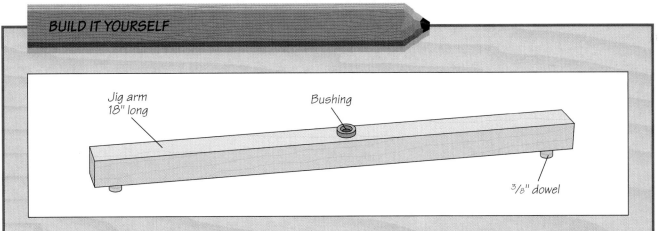

Jig arm
18" long

Bushing

³/₈" dowel

CENTER-DRILLING JIG

To bore holes that are centered on the surface of a board, use the shop-made center-drilling jig shown above. The illustration provides suggested dimensions.

Use a straight piece of 1-by-1 stock for the jig arm. You can make such a device any length you choose, but cutting it to the length shown allows it to accommodate even the widest stock used in a typical project. Mark the center of the top face of the arm and bore a hole through it for a guide bushing. The hole should be ⅛ inch larger in diameter than the bushing, which should be slightly larger than the holes you wish to make with the jig. Press the bushing into place.

Next, turn the arm over and mark a line down the middle. Mark points on the line ¾ inch from each end, then bore holes halfway through the stock at these points, making them large enough to hold a ³/₈-inch grooved dowel. Dab some glue into the holes and insert the dowels.

To use the jig, position it on the stock and pivot the arm until the dowels are up against the opposite edges of the workpiece. Holding the jig with one hand, fit the drill bit into the bushing and bore the hole (below).

For a hole centered on the edge of a board, first secure the workpiece edge-up in a vise. Then position the jig on the edge of the stock with the dowels flush against its opposite faces.

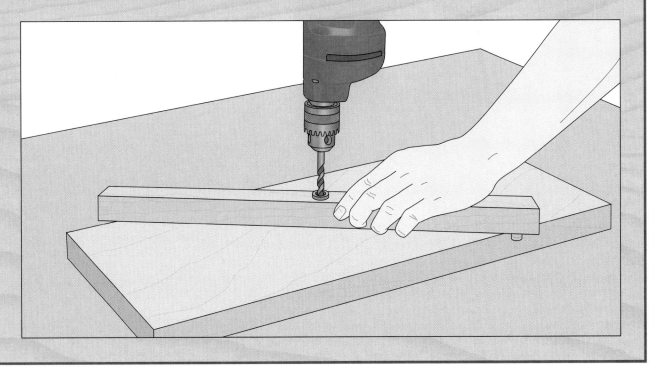

SANDING, SCRAPING AND SMOOTHING

Coupled with a sanding drum, flap sander, or rasp, your drill can perform many tasks, from smoothing stock to shaping contoured edges. As illustrated below, you can bring the drill to the job or, if you prefer to feed the stock into the tool, mount the drill in a stand, transforming it into a stationary sander. If you are holding the tool by hand, make sure you clamp the stock to a work surface to keep it steady during the sanding operation.

Sanding drums are ideal for smoothing curved edges. Often sold in sets, the drums typically consist of replaceable sanding sleeves that fit tightly around solid rubber ones, ranging in diameter from ½ inch to 3 inches.

Flap sanders are made up of abrasive strips with pliable brush backing that

Mounted in a stand and fitted with a flap sander, an electric drill becomes a stationary sander, ideal for smoothing the contours of a cabriole leg.

can be forced into corners and small openings. Unscored strips are best for flat surfaces, while scored strips work well on contours. Whichever sanding accessory you insert in your drill, use a fast drill speed along with a light feed pressure. The finer the grit of the abrasive, the faster the drill speed should be.

For quick stock removal, use a rotary or disk rasp. The type or shape of rasp you choose will depend on the job at hand. Cylindrical rasps are ideal for forming edges and corners, while conical rasps work best in tight spots. Disk rasps are for use on flat surfaces.

As with sanding drums, rasps should be applied only with light feed pressure. Too much force will cause a buildup of heat, possibly burning the surface of the stock and clogging the teeth of the rasp.

SANDING AND SMOOTHING STOCK

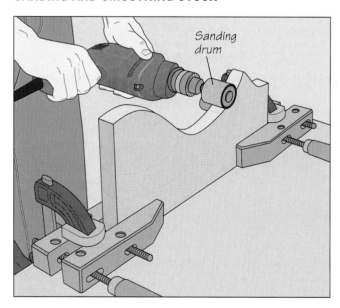

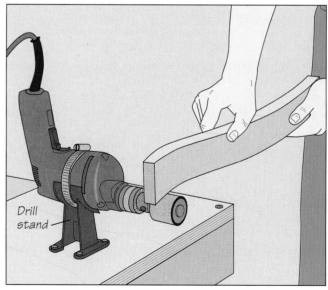

Using a drum sander
Holding the drill parallel to the surface to be sanded, turn on the power and move the sanding drum from left to right while applying light pressure *(above, left)*. To produce a more even finish and prolong the life of the sanding sleeve, reverse the direction of the drill's motor midway through the operation; finish the job sanding from right to left. For a workpiece that is awkward to clamp down, you may prefer to use a commercial drill stand. Screw the stand to a plywood base, then attach the drill. Lock the motor in the On position, then feed the stock across the sleeve against the direction of drum rotation *(above, right)*. Once again, switch the direction of the motor at some point during the process.

SANDING DISK TABLE

To use your drill as a stationary sander, construct a sanding disk table for your tool from ¾-inch plywood. The table will allow you to feed stock into the rotating abrasive surface in a controlled fashion, keeping the workpiece square to the tool. Refer to the illustration at right for suggested dimensions.

Cut a notch in the edge of the jig top that will sit nearest the sanding disk. Temporarily affix the drill stand to the base, then mount the tool in the stand and install the disk in the drill chuck. Trim the two sides so that the upper surface of the table top sits just above the level of the washer on the disk. Screw the sides to the top; if you wish to conceal the screws, counterbore them and cover their heads with wood plugs. Screw the sides to the base.

Position the stand so that the disk will rotate freely within the notch in the top, then screw the stand to the base.

Before beginning to sand, bolt or clamp the table to a work surface. Lock the motor in the On position, then feed the workpiece at a uniform speed across the disk, working against the direction of drill rotation *(right, below)*. Avoid burning or gouging the wood by feeding the stock with one smooth, continuous motion. To even out wear of the sanding disk, reverse the direction of the drill motor midway through the operation, and feed the stock from the other side of the table.

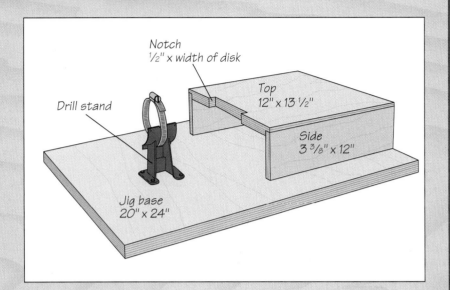

Notch
½" x width of disk

Top
12" x 13 ½"

Drill stand

Side
3 ⅜" x 12"

Jig base
20" x 24"

Sanding disk

SCRAPING AND SURFACING STOCK

Working with a rotary rasp

A rotary rasp is an effective tool for roughing out decorative curves along the edges of a workpiece. To cut a tight curve, hold the drill with both hands and apply moderate pressure to the surface until the rasp cuts the shape you need *(right)*. To rough out a gentle curve, press more lightly and move the rasp along the wood surface, proceeding opposite the direction of drill rotation.

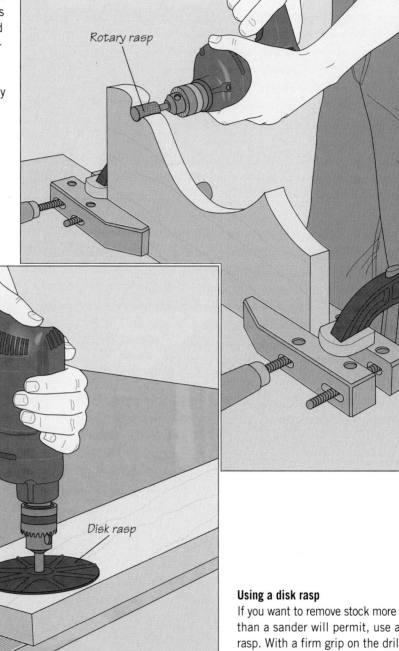

Rotary rasp

Disk rasp

Using a disk rasp

If you want to remove stock more quickly than a sander will permit, use a disk rasp. With a firm grip on the drill, hold the tool perpendicular to the surface, applying only enough pressure to allow the rasp teeth to cut into the wood. (Too much pressure may cause the disk to bite too deeply into the wood, stalling the drill motor.) Move the tool across the surface following the grain of the wood.

THE PORTABLE DRILL AS DRILL PRESS

If your workshop does not include a drill press, and you have no immediate plans to buy one, mounting your portable tool in a drill press stand can provide some of the capabilities of the stationary tool. Naturally, such a compromise solution cannot rival the real thing when it comes to precision and versatility. Depending on your needs, however, a drill press stand may serve you just fine, and you will probably find that it allows you to do some jobs much better than if you had been holding the drill in your hand.

With the added stability afforded by the stand, you can install a small-diameter Forstner bit in the drill and produce perfectly perpendicular, flat-bottomed holes. Most stands include a depth adjustment feature, useful if you want

to bore a uniform series of holes. In selecting a stand, keep in mind that some models can accommodate any make of drill while others will only accept certain varieties.

For convenience and maximum stability, bolt your drill press stand to a base of ¾-inch plywood, then clamp the base to a work surface.

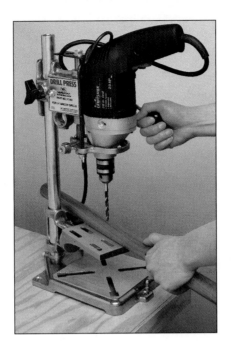

With a tiltable work table, this drill press stand enables a portable drill to bore precise angled holes. The V-groove in the table is designed to hold a cylinder securely.

BORING HOLES

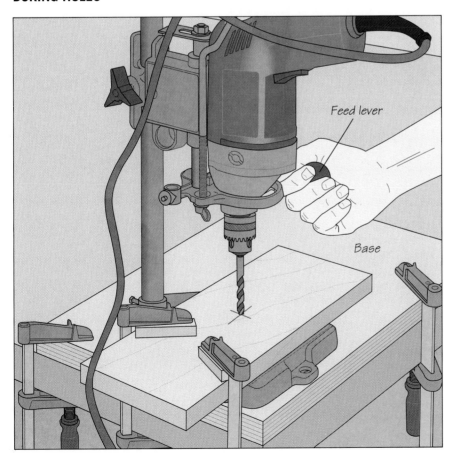

Feed lever

Base

Drilling with a commercial stand
Install a bit in the drill and mount the tool in the stand following the manufacturer's instructions. Set your stock on the table of the stand and align the drilling mark directly under the bit before clamping the workpiece in place. If you are boring a stopped hole, set the drilling depth. Lock the motor in the On position, then rotate the feed lever steadily to feed the bit into the workpiece *(left)*.

ROUTER

A router can fashion more joints than any other portable power tool. Here, one is used to shape a tenon at the end of a board, aided by a mortise-and-tenon jig.

Comprising little more than a base plate and a motor that spins a cutting edge, the router's simplicity belies its versatility. Unlike other portable power tools, the router has no stationary counterpart that can outperform it. As such, the router is a must-have tool for most woodworkers; some claim that it is the single most important shop tool invention of the twentieth century. The earliest model, developed during the First World War, featured a cutter created from the worm gear of an electric barber's clipper. Within 10 years, more than 100,000 "Electric Hand Shapers" had been produced.

Shaping the edge of a workpiece with a decorative profile is probably the router's most common task. It can do the job as reliably on a circular workpiece as on a straight board. The great number of bits available—from rabbet and chamfering cutters to corner round and beading bits—allows you to create dozens of distinctive profiles. There are also a number of accessories designed to keep the cut consistent from the beginning of a pass to the end. For straight cuts, an edge guide keeps the bit from veering off the cutting path *(page 79)*. For shaping the circumference of a circle, or cutting out a circle, special guides will hold the bit a uniform distance from the center *(page 85)*, ensuring perfect results. Both types of guides can be purchased, but you can also make them in the shop.

Mounting the router in a table transforms it into a stationary tool and frees your hands for feeding stock into the bit. You can also install certain bits in a table-mounted router that offer profiles you cannot use when operating the router by hand. A table also makes the router an excellent tool for cutting joints *(page 97)*, including the tongue-and-groove and the sliding dovetail. But with one of the many commercial jigs on the market, you can produce accurate mortise-and-tenon joints and dovetail joints with a hand-held router.

Despite the various design differences, all routers fall into two basic categories: standard and plunge models. The main difference between them has to do with the way the bit bites into the wood at the beginning of a stopped-groove cut. The base plate of a standard router must be held at an angle to the surface so that the bit can be lowered gradually into the wood. The plunge router can be held flat on the surface before the cut since the entire motor assembly, along with the bit, is mounted above the base on spring-loaded columns. Downward pressure on the handles feeds the bit into the wood.

A dovetail bit carves a channel in a hardwood panel. Running the router base plate along a guide keeps the cut square to the edges of the boards. The joint is a good one for installing shelves in a bookcase.

ANATOMY OF A ROUTER

While all routers are designed to spin bits, no two makes or models share exactly the same features or design. Some of the differences, such as the location of the On/off switch, are strictly a matter of convenience or personal preference; other variations determine the kind of work you can perform with the tool.

The collets of many smaller routers only accept bits with ¼-inch-diameter shanks. Larger models can also accommodate ⅜- or ½-inch cutters. Tool power and bit capacity typically go hand in hand. Smaller routers start at ½ horsepower, while manufacturers claim as much as 3 horsepower for some larger models. Greater power enables a router to turn larger bits and make deeper cuts, so it is worth buying a tool with at least 1 horsepower.

Many routers feature variable speed control, which enables you to match the bit speed to the job at hand. Depending on the model, you can set the speed at levels between 8,000 and 24,000 rpm. Slow speeds are best for deep cuts such as when you are using a panel-raising bit; very high speeds come in handy for jobs such as trimming laminate. In general, high speed will produce a cleaner

STANDARD ROUTER

On/off switch

Base plate clamp screw
Loosened to set cutting depth of bit or remove base plate from body; tightened to lock plate in position

Depth adjustment ring
Used for setting cutting depth of bit

Base plate
Supports motor. Removable for bit changing or for mounting router in table; adjustable for setting cutting depth

Handle

Collet
Jaws accept shank of router bit; nut directly above collet is turned to open or close jaws to secure cutter in place

Sub-base
Screw holes allow accessories to be attached to router; can be unscrewed from the base plate.

PORTER+CABLE

cut. Its one drawback is the increased risk of burning.

While some routers, like the one featured on page 70, include a plunge base *(below)* that can be added to the standard machine, you can also buy a tool specifically designed for plunge routing. Pressing down on the handles plunges the bit directly into the stock—ideal if you have to start a cut in the middle of a workpiece.

PLUNGE BASE

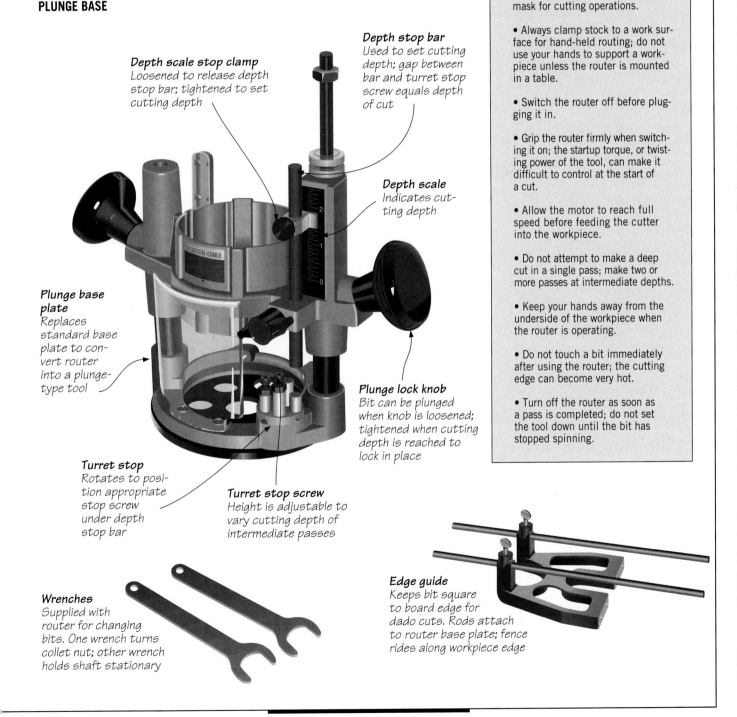

Depth scale stop clamp
Loosened to release depth stop bar; tightened to set cutting depth

Depth stop bar
Used to set cutting depth; gap between bar and turret stop screw equals depth of cut

Depth scale
Indicates cutting depth

Plunge base plate
Replaces standard base plate to convert router into a plunge-type tool

Turret stop
Rotates to position appropriate stop screw under depth stop bar

Turret stop screw
Height is adjustable to vary cutting depth of intermediate passes

Plunge lock knob
Bit can be plunged when knob is loosened; tightened when cutting depth is reached to lock in place

Wrenches
Supplied with router for changing bits. One wrench turns collet nut; other wrench holds shaft stationary

Edge guide
Keeps bit square to board edge for dado cuts. Rods attach to router base plate; fence rides along workpiece edge

ROUTER SAFETY TIPS

- Keep router bits clean and sharp; replace any damaged cutters.

- Unplug the router before changing a bit.

- Wear safety glasses and a dust mask for cutting operations.

- Always clamp stock to a work surface for hand-held routing; do not use your hands to support a workpiece unless the router is mounted in a table.

- Switch the router off before plugging it in.

- Grip the router firmly when switching it on; the startup torque, or twisting power of the tool, can make it difficult to control at the start of a cut.

- Allow the motor to reach full speed before feeding the cutter into the workpiece.

- Do not attempt to make a deep cut in a single pass; make two or more passes at intermediate depths.

- Keep your hands away from the underside of the workpiece when the router is operating.

- Do not touch a bit immediately after using the router; the cutting edge can become very hot.

- Turn off the router as soon as a pass is completed; do not set the tool down until the bit has stopped spinning.

BITS

Fitted with the right bit for the job at hand, a router can cut anything from a rabbet to an intricate molded edge. The selection of cutters available today is very broad. Some tool and hardware catalogs boast page after page of router bits, with scores of different profiles—each available in several cutting diameters. No matter what kind of cut you have in mind, you can almost always find the appropriate bit.

Standard bits for portable routers consist of a steel body with one or more cutting surfaces and a shank that fits into the collet. Cutters for this tool are generally available in two materials: high-speed steel (HSS) and high-speed steel with carbide cutting edges. Although carbide-tipped bits are more expensive, they stay sharp longer and cut more easily through tough materials. One drawback, however, is that they tend to chip if they strike a hard surface.

Router bits fall into two categories; those for shaping edges and those for cutting grooves. As their name implies, edge-forming bits are used to cut decorative profiles into stock or prepare board edges for joinery. These bits generally have a pilot located below the cutter to ride along the edge of the workpiece and guide the bit. Ball-bearing pilots are preferable to fixed pilots because they do not generate heat from friction and thus will not cause burns or compression marks on your stock. Grooving bits are used for making dadoes. If the dado will not run to the edge of the stock, a plunge router is the best choice.

Your router's performance will benefit from proper storage and careful maintenance of your bits. Use a clean cloth to wipe off dust and dirt. Protect bits from damage in a simple-to-make holder *(page 74)*. Keep the edges sharp and avoid using cutters that are dirty, rusted or damaged. Be sure to unplug the tool whenever you change a bit.

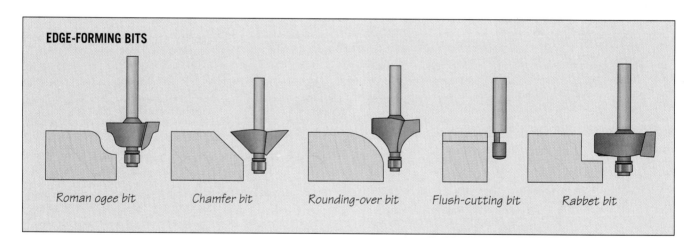

EDGE-FORMING BITS

Roman ogee bit · Chamfer bit · Rounding-over bit · Flush-cutting bit · Rabbet bit

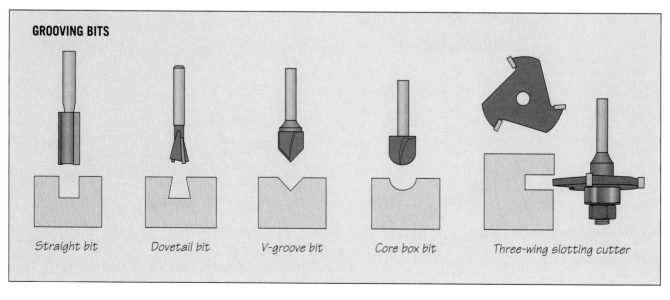

GROOVING BITS

Straight bit · Dovetail bit · V-groove bit · Core box bit · Three-wing slotting cutter

SHOP TIP

Maintaining and replacing pilot bearings

Accumulated dirt will eventually jam the pilot bearing of a router bit. This may lead to burning of the stock. To service a pilot bearing, secure the bit bearing-end up in a vise or handscrews. Wipe off burn marks, pitch and gum with a cloth and an oil-free, non-silicone-based lubricant. If the pilot is damaged or worn—or if you want to alter the bit's cutting profile—replace the pilot by loosening its setscrew with a hex wrench. Remove the pilot and install a new one.

CHANGING A BIT

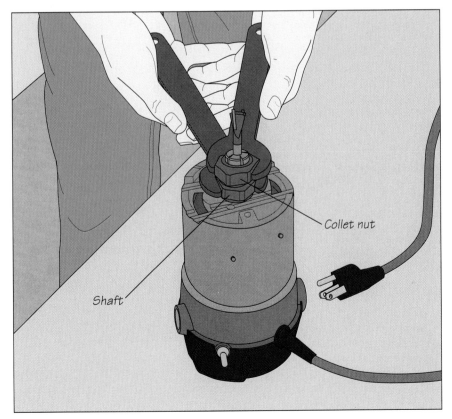

Collet nut

Shaft

Removing and installing bits

Set the router upside down on a work surface and loosen the clamp screw to remove the base plate. Change bits using the two wrenches supplied with the machine. To remove a cutter, hold the shaft steady with one wrench and loosen the collet with the other tool. For extra leverage, position the wrenches so that you can squeeze them together *(left)*. Pull the bit out of the collet; if it is stuck, gently tap the collet with the wrench. Do not strike the bit or try to extract it from the collet with pliers; this may damage the cutting edge. Before installing a new bit, clean any sawdust from the collet. Insert the replacement all the way into the collet, then raise it about $1/16$ inch. Then retighten the collet.

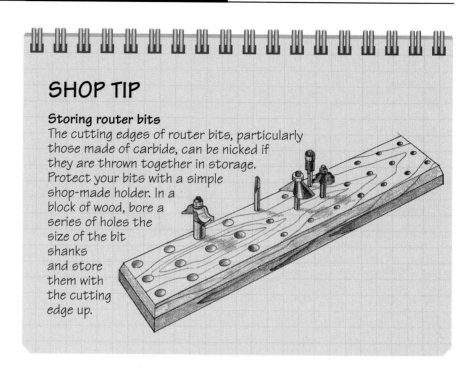

SHOP TIP

Storing router bits
The cutting edges of router bits, particularly those made of carbide, can be nicked if they are thrown together in storage. Protect your bits with a simple shop-made holder. In a block of wood, bore a series of holes the size of the bit shanks and store them with the cutting edge up.

SETTING THE CUTTING DEPTH

Adjusting a standard router

Set the router on the workpiece. Loosen the clamp screw with one hand and rotate the motor to raise or lower it, also raising or lowering the bit. For the straight bit shown, align its tip with the depth line, then tighten the clamp screw. An alternative method is to set the router upside down on a work surface, loosen the clamp screw and rotate the base plate until the bit protrudes by the amount you want.

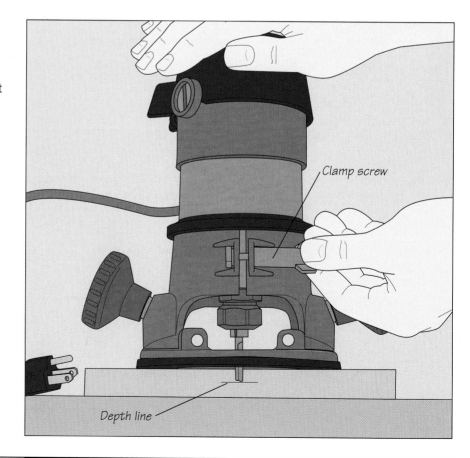

Clamp screw

Depth line

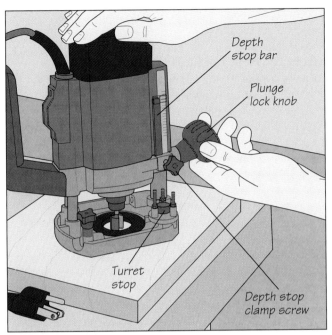

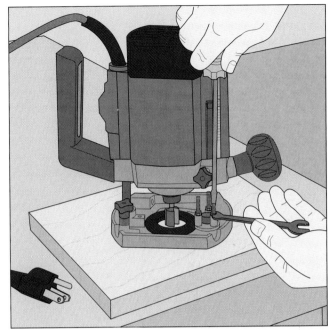

Depth stop bar

Plunge lock knob

Turret stop

Depth stop clamp screw

Adjusting a plunge router

Set the router on the workpiece and rotate the turret stop to position the shortest stop screw directly under the depth stop bar. Loosen the clamp screw to release the bar and seat it on the turret screw. Then loosen the plunge lock knob and push the motor down until the bit contacts the work-piece. Tighten the knob and raise the stop bar until the gap between it and the turret stop screw equals the depth of cut. Tighten the depth stop clamp screw and loosen the plunge lock knob, allowing the motor and bit to spring back up *(above, left)*. When you plunge the bit into the stock, it will penetrate until the bar contacts the turret stop screw. For deep cuts, it is generally preferable to reach your final depth in stages. On the model shown, you can set the height of the other two turret stop screws to make passes at interme-diate depths: loosen the nut with a wrench and then raise or lower the screw with a screwdriver *(above, right)*.

SHOP TIP

An auxiliary sub-base for wider cuts
To make a cut that is wider than a particular router bit, you would normally make one pass, move your edge guide and make a second pass. Instead, use an off-square sub-base. Cut a piece of 1/4-inch plywood into an 8-inch square. Remove the router's sub-base and bore the screw holes and clearance hole for the bit through the auxiliary sub-base. Next, shave 1/16 inch of wood from one edge of the plywood, 1/8 inch from an adjacent edge and 1/4 inch from a third edge. Mark the amounts you removed on each side. Screw the auxiliary base to the router and make a pass with the unshaved edge riding against the guide. Rotate the base and make a second pass that is 1/16, 1/8 or 1/4 inch wider than the first, depending on which edge you use.

ROUTER ACCESSORIES

Since the development of the portable router, an entire segment of the power tool industry has burgeoned. The purpose of the new activity is to design accessories that widen the router's usefulness and enhance its capabilities. The photo below illustrates a few of the more popular devices.

Some of these products, like the foot switch, make the router more convenient to use. The switch is especially handy with routers whose on/off controls are not close to the handles. If you use such a device, be sure to disconnect it from the tool when you are changing a bit or performing any other maintenance operation. This will prevent accidental start-up of the motor.

The edge and circle guide enables a router to cut grooves a set distance in from the workpiece edge, rout a molding or follow the contours of curves. As shown on page 86, the jig also can be used to keep a router bit a uniform distance from the center of a workpiece, ensuring accurate circle cuts.

The dovetail jig is one of several accessories designed to make the router a key part of the joint-making process. The model shown below features adjustable fingers that allow you to create your own dovetail pattern by varying the widths and spacing of the pins and tails.

A SAMPLING OF ACCESSORIES

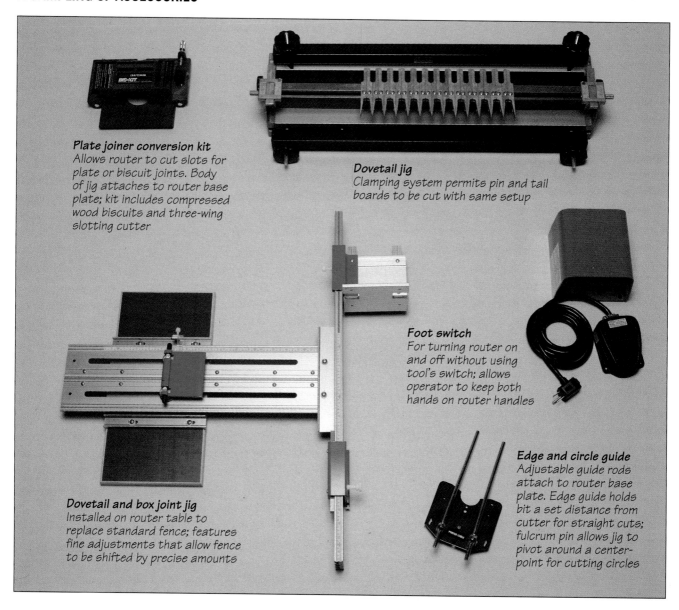

Plate joiner conversion kit
Allows router to cut slots for plate or biscuit joints. Body of jig attaches to router base plate; kit includes compressed wood biscuits and three-wing slotting cutter

Dovetail jig
Clamping system permits pin and tail boards to be cut with same setup

Foot switch
For turning router on and off without using tool's switch; allows operator to keep both hands on router handles

Dovetail and box joint jig
Installed on router table to replace standard fence; features fine adjustments that allow fence to be shifted by precise amounts

Edge and circle guide
Adjustable guide rods attach to router base plate. Edge guide holds bit a set distance from cutter for straight cuts; fulcrum pin allows jig to pivot around a center-point for cutting circles

EDGE FORMING

Whether you are carving a decorative molding into a workpiece or preparing boards for a joint, shaping edges will probably be one of your most common uses of the router. As illustrated in the pages that follow, the manner in which you guide the bit along the stock depends on the type of cutter you are using. With piloted bits, the pilot rides along the edge, keeping penetration of the cutting edges constant. With non-piloted bits, the router base plate runs along an edge guide clamped to the workpiece, achieving the same result. Either method will work on a straight edge, but for a curved cut you will need a piloted bit. One note of caution: Kickback can occur at any time until the pilot contacts the stock. So maintain a firm grasp on the router.

For any routing operation, be aware of the feed direction. As illustrated below, it should generally be counter to the direction of bit rotation. Before starting a cut, clamp your stock to a work surface and make sure that the clamps will not get in the way of the router.

An edge-forming bit etches a decorative profile on the circumference of a table top. The cutter's ball-bearing pilot rides along the stock to keep the cut at a uniform depth.

ROUTER FEED DIRECTION

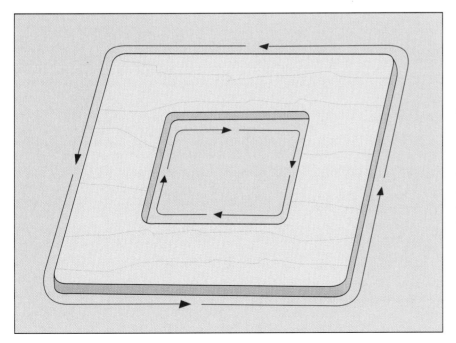

Feeding the router
Moving the router in the wrong direction can make the tool difficult to control, resulting in kickback and tearout. For most operations, guide the bit into a workpiece against the direction of bit rotation; this will tend to pull the bit into the wood. On an outside edge, move the router in a counterclockwise direction; on an inside edge, feed the tool clockwise *(left)*. Start with cuts that are against the grain; this way, you will be able to eliminate any tearout with the cuts along the grain that follow. Position yourself so that you can pull the router toward you, rather than having to push it; this will enable you to see the bit at all times. Throughout the operation, maintain a firm hold on the tool and apply moderate pressure to keep the bit biting into the wood.

STRAIGHT AND CURVED CUTS

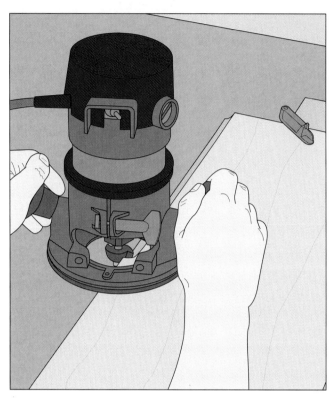

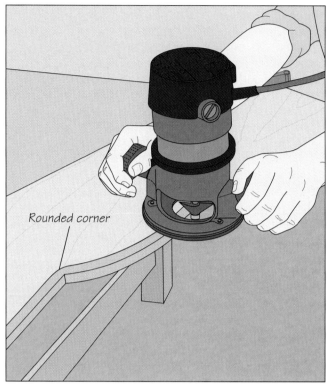

Rounded corner

Routing with a piloted bit

Clamp your stock to a work surface with the edge you want to shape extending off the table by several inches. Holding the router with both hands, rest its base plate on the workpiece at one end with the bit clear of the wood and turn on the tool. Ease the bit into the stock until the pilot contacts the edge, keeping the base plate flat on the workpiece *(above, left)*. For deep cuts, make two or more passes to reach your final depth. On a curved cut, the router bit will round off any inside corners along the edge of the workpiece *(above, right)*; square these corners with a chisel.

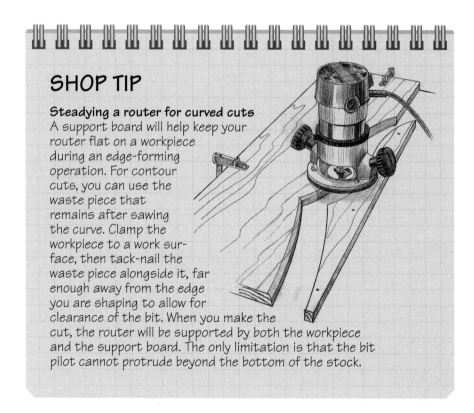

SHOP TIP

Steadying a router for curved cuts

A support board will help keep your router flat on a workpiece during an edge-forming operation. For contour cuts, you can use the waste piece that remains after sawing the curve. Clamp the workpiece to a work surface, then tack-nail the waste piece alongside it, far enough away from the edge you are shaping to allow for clearance of the bit. When you make the cut, the router will be supported by both the workpiece and the support board. The only limitation is that the bit pilot cannot protrude beyond the bottom of the stock.

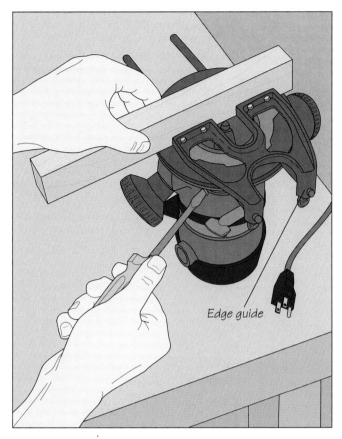

Edge guide

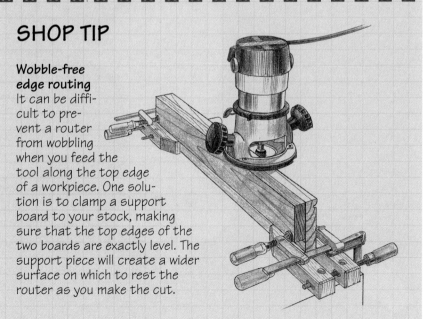

SHOP TIP

Wobble-free edge routing
It can be difficult to prevent a router from wobbling when you feed the tool along the top edge of a workpiece. One solution is to clamp a support board to your stock, making sure that the top edges of the two boards are exactly level. The support piece will create a wider surface on which to rest the router as you make the cut.

Using a non-piloted bit
To prepare for the cut, install a commercial edge guide on the router. Set the tool upside down on a work surface and insert the rods of the guide into the predrilled holes in the router base plate. Hold a scrap board on the bit to help you position the guide for the width of cut, then butt its fence against the board. Tighten the screws in the router base plate to fix the guide in position *(above, left)*. To make the cut, clamp your stock to the work surface. Then, keeping the guide fence flush against the edge you wish to shape, start the cut at one end of the workpiece and feed the router along the board edge *(above, right)* until you reach the other end.

MAKING A STOPPED RABBET

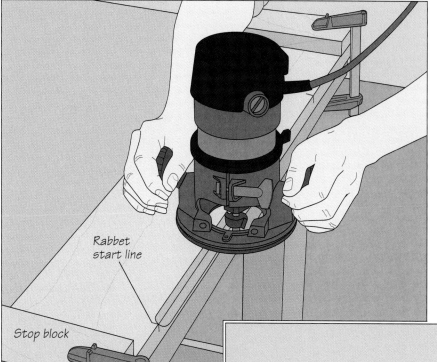

Rabbet start line

Stop block

Cutting with a piloted bit

Set your stock on a work surface and mark lines for the beginning and end of the stopped rabbet on the edge you wish to cut. Align the rabbetting bit with one of the marks and clamp a board as a stop block to the workpiece flush against the router base plate. Then line up the bit with the other mark and clamp another stop guide in place. Gripping the router firmly with both hands, butt its base plate against one stop block and guide the bit into the stock at the rabbet start line. Continue the cut along the edge until the base plate touches the other stop block.

Using a non-piloted bit

Clamp your stock to a work surface, then mark a line for the end of the stopped rabbet on the edge of the workpiece. (The rabbet shown in the illustration is stopped at only one end.) Align the bit on the top face of the stock for the width of the rabbet, then clamp an edge guide to the workpiece flush against the router base plate. With a firm grip on the router, feed the bit into the stock at the starting end of the rabbet, butting the router base plate against the edge guide. Then feed the bit along the edge of the workpiece, keeping the base plate flush against the guide *(right)*. Stop the cut when the bit reaches the rabbet end line.

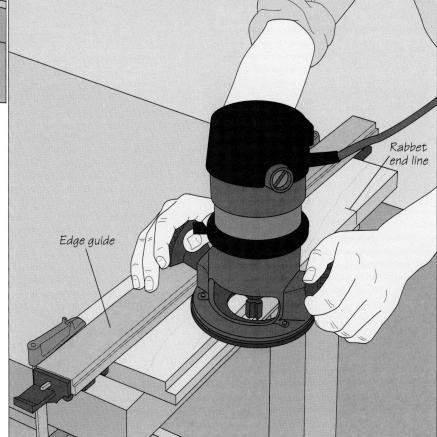

Rabbet end line

Edge guide

DADO CUTS

Although any router can be used to make dado cuts, it is much easier to cut channels that stop in the middle of a workpiece if you have access to a plunge router. With the tool flat on your workpiece, you simply press the bit straight down into the wood and feed it to the end of the cut. With a standard router, you need to raise the bit clear of the stock and pivot it into the wood. In either case, the end of the stopped dado or groove will be rounded and will have to be squared off with a chisel.

Most dado cuts are made with straight bits. The maximum depth of a single pass will depend on the hardness

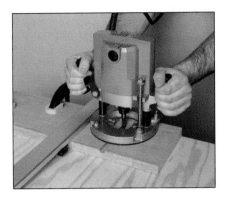

A grooving bit carves a dado in a board. Riding the router base plate along an edge guide produces a cut perpendicular to the board edges.

of the wood you are milling and the power of your router. As a rule of thumb, make several passes for deep channels in hardwood. For cuts whose width exceeds the diameter of the bits you have on hand, make two or more passes, repositioning your edge guide after each pass by an amount equal to the bit diameter. Three adjacent passes with a ¼-inch bit, for example, will yield a ¾-inch-wide dado or groove.

As shown below, the edge guide supplied with routers is a handy prop for cuts close to the edge or end of a workpiece. But you can easily set up a guide for cuts that are farther in from the sides.

MAKING A DADO CUT

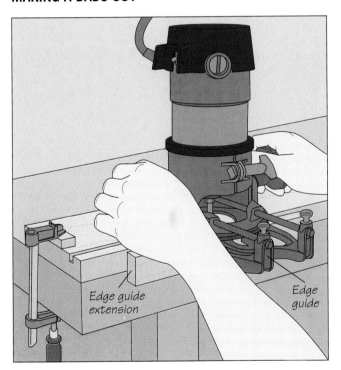

Edge guide extension

Edge guide

Cutting a groove
Make a cutting mark for the groove on the face of the workpiece, then screw a board to a commercial edge guide to serve as an extension. Align the bit with the cutting mark and install the guide on your router so that the extension is flush against the edge of the workpiece. Starting at one end of the board, feed the bit into the stock with the edge guide extension flat against the edge of the stock. Continue the cut until you reach the other end, repositioning your clamps as necessary.

Edge guide

Routing a dado
Set your stock on a work surface and make a cutting mark for the dado on its face. Align the bit with the mark and clamp a board as an edge guide to the workpiece flush against the router base plate. The board should be longer than the width of your workpiece; make sure that it is square to the edges of the stock. Grip the router firmly with both hands and butt its base plate against the edge guide. Feed the bit into the stock at the cutting line and make the cut.

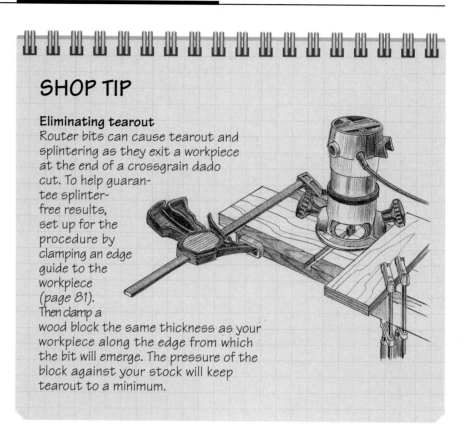

SHOP TIP

Eliminating tearout
Router bits can cause tearout and splintering as they exit a workpiece at the end of a crossgrain dado cut. To help guarantee splinter-free results, set up for the procedure by clamping an edge guide to the workpiece (page 81). Then clamp a wood block the same thickness as your workpiece along the edge from which the bit will emerge. The pressure of the block against your stock will keep tearout to a minimum.

BUILD IT YOURSELF

T-SQUARE JIG FOR DADO CUTS
The T-square at right will make quick work of dadoes and grooves. Built from ¾-inch plywood, the jig ensures that dado cuts will be square to the edges of your stock.

The dimensions of the jig depend on the width of the stock you will be using and the diameter of your router base plate. Make the edge guide at least as long as the workpiece is wide. The fence should be about 4 inches wide and long enough to clamp to the stock without getting in the way of the

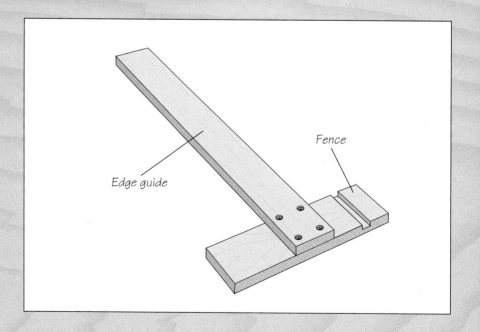

Fence

Edge guide

MAKING A STOPPED GROOVE

1 Plunging the bit into the stock
Set the stock on a work surface, then align the bit with one edge of the outline. Clamp a board as a stop block to the work-piece flush with the router base plate. Repeat on the other edges until you have a stop block on all four sides of the out-line. To start the cut with a plunge router, set the tool flat on the workpiece with the bit above the outline and clear of the stock. Then loosen the plunge lock knob, turn the router on and use both hands to plunge the bit into the stock *(right)*. Once the bit reaches the required depth, lock the knob. To start the cut with a standard router, rest its sub-base on the workpiece with the bit clear of the stock and above the outline *(inset)*. Then, gripping the tool firmly, turn it on and lower the bit into the workpiece until the sub-base is flat on the surface.

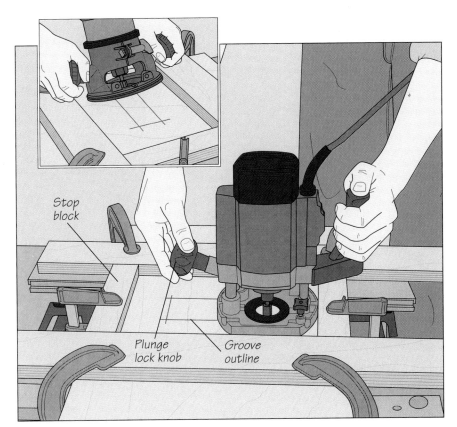

Stop block

Plunge lock knob

Groove outline

router. Screw the two parts of the jig together, checking with a try square to make certain that they are perfect-ly perpendicular to each other. Then clamp the T-square to a work sur-face and rout a dado across the fence. Keep the router base plate butted against the edge guide as you make the cut.

To use the jig, clamp it to the workpiece with the dado in the fence aligned with the cutting mark on the stock. Make the cut, pressing the router base plate firmly against the edge guide *(right)*.

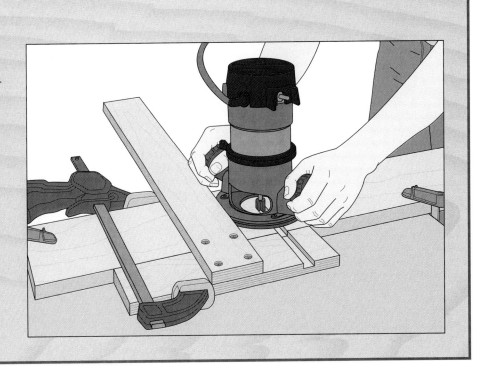

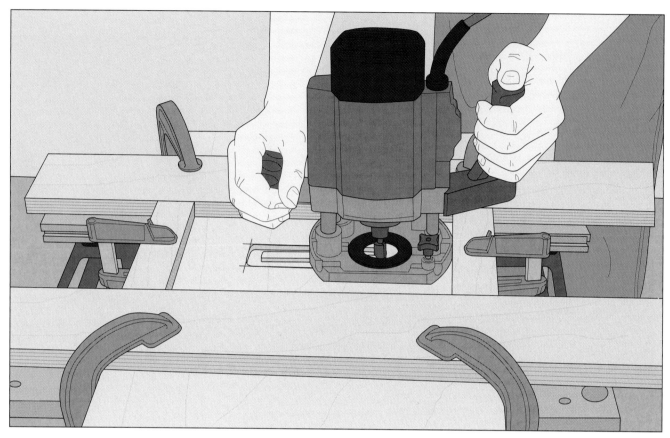

2 Completing the groove
Guide the router in a clockwise direction to cut the outside edges of the groove, keeping the base plate flush against a stop block at all times *(above)*. To complete the groove, rout out the remaining waste, feeding the tool against the direction of bit rotation as much as possible.

SHOP TIP

Routing two dadoes in a single pass
For a shelf to sit level in a carcase, it must rest in dadoes at the same height in both side panels. One way to ensure that the cuts will match up is to rout the two dadoes at the same time. Clamp your stock to a work surface, making sure that the ends of the boards are aligned. Then line up the dadoes you wish to cut with the pre-cut channel in the fence of a T-square jig (page 82), and complete the job in a single pass.

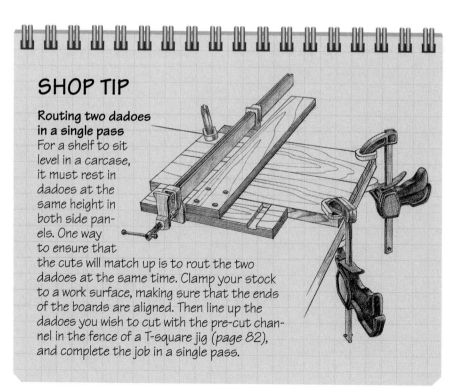

ROUTING CIRCLES

Aided by a guide that keeps the bit a set distance from a centerpoint, your router can cut arcs and circles or add a decorative flourish by carving rings in a workpiece. Different styles of guides are available, but sometimes you can make do with the edge guide supplied with your router. Some woodworkers even improvise with a chain tether attached to the tool's handle.

While commercial guides can be adjusted to cut circles of varying diameters, the length of some guides will limit the size of your circles. You can always use a shop-built jig, however, to rout larger disks (pages 86 and 87).

As with the cutting of dadoes, plunge routers are more convenient than their standard counterparts for circle cutting. For through cuts, to prevent the bit from marring your work surface when it finishes severing the circle, work atop a thin sheet of scrap wood. You can also shift the workpiece so that the part being routed sticks over the edge of the work surface as you complete the cut.

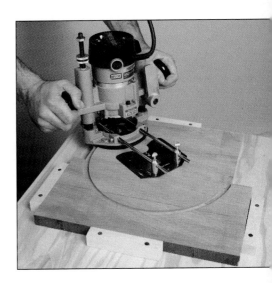

Attached to a commercial guide, a router can sever circles from stock—ideal for forming tabletops and stool seats.

CUTTING A CIRCLE

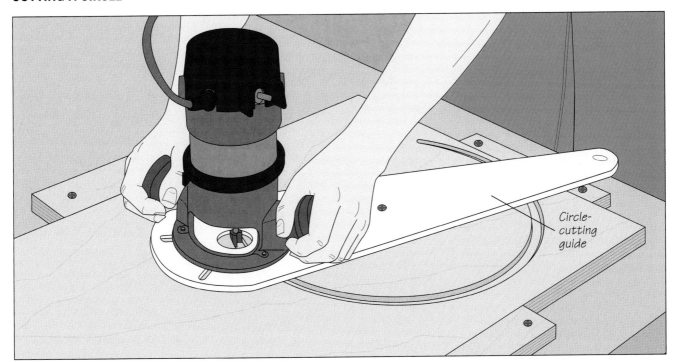

Circle-cutting guide

Using a standard router

Set your stock on a work surface. Butt wood scraps against the edges of the workpiece to act as stop blocks, then nail them in place. Install a straight bit in the router. To attach the commercial circle-cutting guide shown, remove the tool's subbase, then screw the guide to the base plate through the predrilled holes. Determine the radius of the circle you wish to cut—the distance between the circumference and the center—and mark this length on the guide, measuring from the center of the bit. Drill a hole through the guide at the center of the circle, halfway between the edges of the jig. Then screw it to the workpiece until it is secure but still able to swivel. Gripping the router firmly, tilt the tool until the bit is clear of the stock. Turn it on and lower the cutter into the workpiece until the guide is flat on the surface. Move the router clockwise, readjusting the cutting depth as necessary until you finish routing the circle.

Working with a plunge router

Set up your stock and router as you would for working with a standard router *(page 85)*, then mark the radius of the circle and mark its centerpoint. For a deep cut, set the cutting depth so that you can gradually reach the final depth with two or more passes. Fix the pivot point of a commercial circle-cutting guide to the center of the circle, then install the guide on the router so that the bit is aligned with the radius mark. With the cutter clear of the workpiece, grip the router firmly and plunge the bit into the stock. Feed the tool steadily in a clockwise direction until the circle is completed, keeping the router flat on the workpiece throughout the operation.

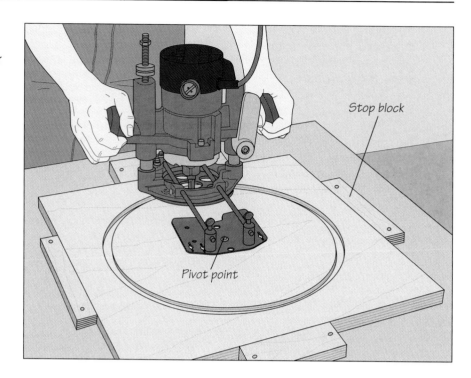

Stop block

Pivot point

BUILD IT YOURSELF

ADJUSTABLE CIRCLE-CUTTING JIG

For cutting circles of different sizes, use the shop-made jig shown at right. Refer to the illustration for suggested dimensions of the center block. The diameter of the dowels depends on the size of the predrilled slots in the base plate of your router; make the wooden rods at least as long as the radius of the largest circle you expect to cut.

To assemble the jig, insert the dowels into the slots on the router, then set the tool flat on a work surface. Butt one edge of the center block against the ends of the dowels and mark the two points where they touch. At each spot, bore a hole at least halfway through the block with a drill bit the same diameter as the dowels. Dab some glue into the holes and insert the dowels, then

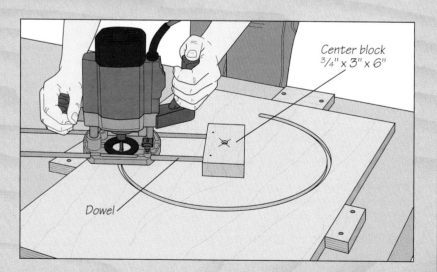

Center block
³/₄" x 3" x 6"

Dowel

fix them in place with small finishing nails. Next, mark the center of the block and bore a hole through it for a screw.

Use the jig as you would a commercial circle-cutting guide *(above)*.

Screw the block to the center of the circle and slide the dowels along the router base plate until the bit is aligned with the outline. Then rout the circle, feeding the router in a clockwise direction.

COMPASS JIG

The compass jig at right, shop-made from ¼-inch plywood, will enable you to cut larger circles than is possible with most commercial circle-cutting guides. The dimensions of the jig will depend on the size of your router and the radius of the largest circle that you plan to cut. Make the circular part of the jig slightly larger than your tool's base plate. The arm of the jig should be about 2 inches wide and longer than the radius of the circle you will be cutting. Cut out the jig with a band saw or a saber saw, then bore a hole in the center of the rounded end, making it large enough to accommodate the router bit.

To customize the jig for your router, remove the sub-base of the tool and set it on the circular section of the jig. With the bit centered over the hole, mark the positions of the screw holes in the base. Bore the holes and attach the jig to your router. Then draw a line down the center of the jig arm.

To use the jig, determine the radius of the circle you want to cut and transfer this length to the guide, measuring from the center of the bit along the line you have already drawn. Mark a point on the arm for the center of the circle, then bore a hole and screw the jig to the workpiece. Lower the bit into the stock as you would for a commercial guide (page 85) and cut the circle, moving the router in a clockwise direction (right, bottom).

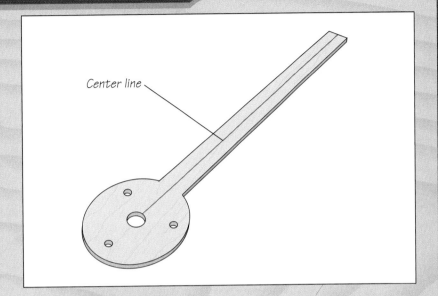

Center line

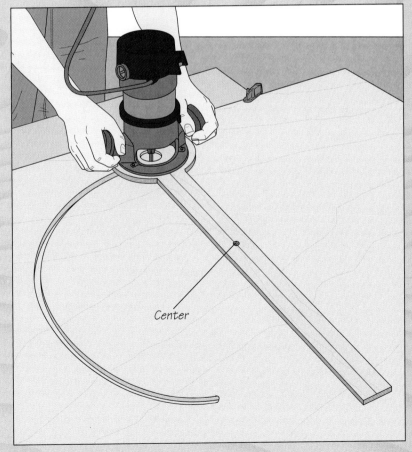

Center

PATTERN ROUTING

Pattern routing is a timesaving method of routing multiple copies of the same contoured shape. The technique involves making a template of the pattern you wish to reproduce, then using the cut-out shape to guide the router bit during subsequent cuts.

The exact procedure you follow will depend on the type of bit you are using. With the non-piloted variety, you need to attach a template guide—a metal collar that surrounds the bit shank, leaving the cutting edges protruding. With the pattern clamped atop the workpiece, the guide rides along the edge of the cut-out while the bit bites into the stock.

With the piloted bit shown, you need only to clamp the template atop your workpiece, since the pilot of a pattern routing bit is above the cutting edges. The pilot will follow the template,

enabling the cutting edge to reproduce the pattern on the workpiece.

Whichever method you use, make the template from durable wood, such as

A pilot bearing follows the curves of a pattern while the straight bit underneath it reproduces the design on a workpiece.

plywood or hardboard. Cut the pattern with a band saw or a saber saw, then carefully sand the edges that will be guiding the router. The template must be smooth since any imperfections will be transferred to your stock. Make the template slightly thicker than the height of the template guide.

One advantage of using piloted bits is that you can make the template precisely the same size as the finished pieces you wish to cut. With a template guide, you will have to compensate for the difference between the bit diameter and the diameter of the template collar.

Pattern routing can be done with either a plunge router or a standard router. If you are working with a plunge model you will need to lock the tool at its proper cutting depth before switching on the motor. For the standard router, set the depth of cut in the regular manner.

ROUTING WITH A TEMPLATE

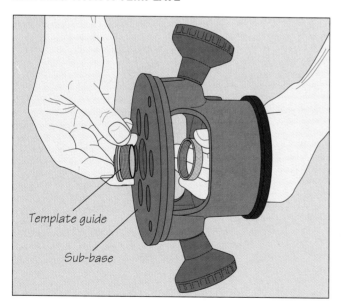

Template guide

Sub-base

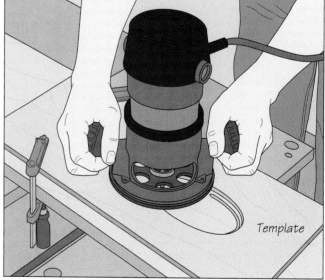

Template

Installing and using a template guide

To install the guide, loosen the clamp screw on the router base plate and remove the plate. Insert the threaded part of the guide through the hole in the middle of the sub-base *(above, left)*, then screw it to the ring to hold the two together; reassemble the router. Set your stock on a work surface and clamp the template on top of it in the desired position. To make the inte-

rior cut shown, plunge the bit into the stock as you would when making a dado cut *(page 83)*, then feed the cutter in a clockwise direction until the guide contacts the template. Complete the cut *(above, right)*, making sure that the guide is always pressed flush against the edge of the pattern throughout the operation.

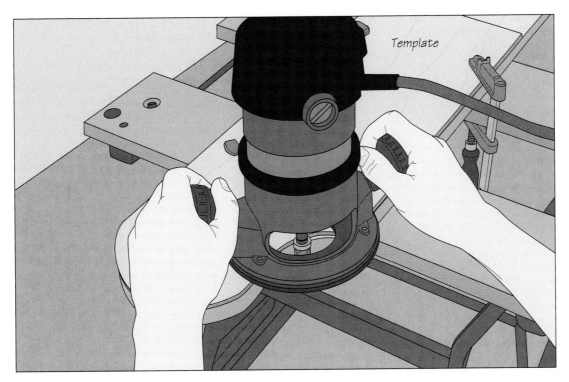

Template

Working with a piloted bit

Use the template to outline the pattern on your workpiece, then cut out most of the waste with a band saw or saber saw, leaving about ⅛ inch of stock outside the cutting line. Place the template on top of your stock and secure the two to a work surface. Cut the pattern as you would when edge forming *(page 78)*, keeping the pilot pressed up against the edge of the template *(above)*.

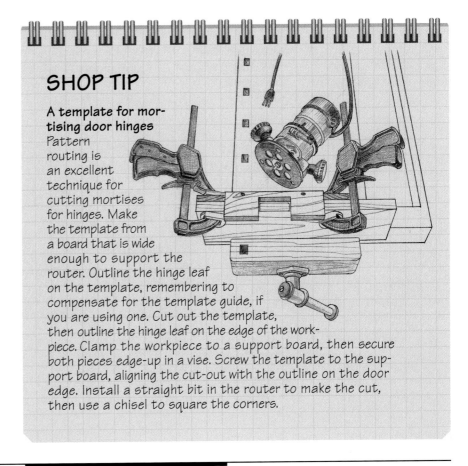

SHOP TIP

A template for mortising door hinges
Pattern routing is an excellent technique for cutting mortises for hinges. Make the template from a board that is wide enough to support the router. Outline the hinge leaf on the template, remembering to compensate for the template guide, if you are using one. Cut out the template, then outline the hinge leaf on the edge of the workpiece. Clamp the workpiece to a support board, then secure both pieces edge-up in a vise. Screw the template to the support board, aligning the cut-out with the outline on the door edge. Install a straight bit in the router to make the cut, then use a chisel to square the corners.

THE ROUTER AS SHAPER

With its bit whirring at 20,000 rpm or faster, the router can be somewhat intimidating. Among the many benefits of installing your router in a table is the extra margin of safety such an arrangement provides. Solidly mounted to a table with its bit barely projecting above the work surface, the router seems much more manageable.

The router table adds a range of versatility that no other single accessory can provide. Among other things, it frees your hands to feed stock into the tool, allowing you to exert greater control on the cutting operation. In addition, there are bits that can only be used on a table-mounted router. While some of the cutters shown in the illustration below—the beading bit, for instance—can also be used in hand-held work, router table bits are generally significantly larger, giving you much greater flexibility when preparing stock for joinery or cutting decorative shapes.

Commercial router tables are available in many sizes and configurations. All models have a guard to cover the bit; many feature an adjustable fence and a groove for a miter gauge. Cutting depth on a router table depends on how far the bit protrudes; the width of cut will depend on how much of the bit extends beyond the fence. On commercial tables, the fence is commonly split. The two halves are normally left in alignment for shallow cuts; the outfeed fence can be set behind the infeed fence for more aggressive removal of stock. For a customized router table, you can also build your own (page 94).

Fitted with a chamfering bit and suspended upside down in a specially designed table, a router becomes a stationary tool—in this case, cutting a decorative V-groove for a tongue-and-groove joint.

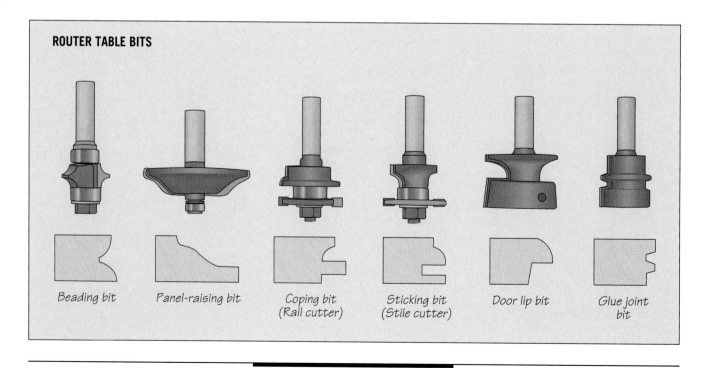

ROUTER TABLE BITS

Beading bit   Panel-raising bit   Coping bit (Rail cutter)   Sticking bit (Stile cutter)   Door lip bit   Glue joint bit

SETTING UP A ROUTER TABLE

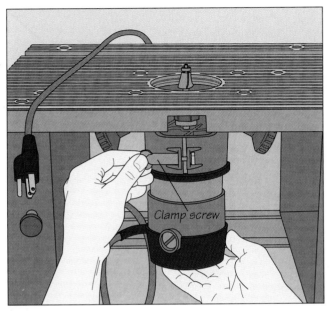

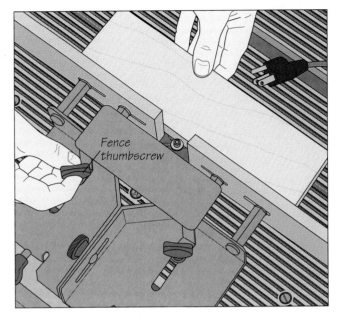

1 Mounting the router in the table
Install your router in a table following the manufacturer's instructions. For the model shown, loosen the clamp screw on the router base plate and remove the plate from the body of the tool. Unscrew the sub-base and fasten the base plate to the underside of the router table, aligning the predrilled holes in the plate with those in the table. Install a bit in the router, then screw the body of the tool into the base plate. Tighten the clamp screw *(above)*.

2 Adjusting the fence
Loosen the four adjustment screws and move the two halves of the fence as close as possible to the bit without touching the cutting edges. Tighten the screws, then set the width of cut, moving the fence back from the bit for a wide cut and advancing it for a shallow pass. For a cutting width equal to the diameter of the piloted panel-raising bit shown *(page 90)*, loosen the four thumbscrews behind the fence. Then hold a straight board against the fence and move both halves together until the board contacts the pilot *(above)*. Tighten the thumbscrews.

ROUTING A MOLDING

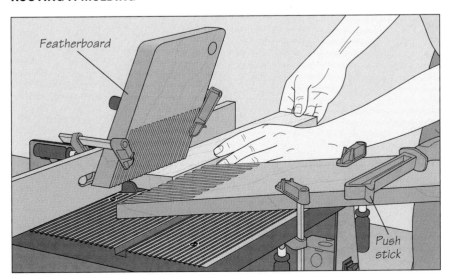

Making the pass
To hold the workpiece in place, clamp two featherboards to the table as shown. Be sure to feed the stock into the cutter against the direction of bit rotation. With your workpiece clear of the bit, turn on the router and slowly feed the stock into the cutting edge while holding it flush against the fence. To keep your hands safely away from the bit, finish the pass with a push stick. Position the safety guard over the bit whenever possible.

ROUTER TABLE MITER GAUGE

If you do not have a miter gauge or if your router table does not have a slot for one, use the shop-made jig shown at right to guide stock accurately across the table. This device is especially helpful for keeping long, narrow boards perpendicular to the fence while cutting into their ends. Since the fence butts against the workpiece, the jig also helps to reduce tearout.

The dimensions of the jig will depend on the size of your table, but those suggested in the illustration are suitable for most commercial models. The length of the gauge—less the thickness of the guide—should not exceed the distance between the bit's pilot and the edge of the table.

To assemble the jig, screw together the gauge and support board, making sure that they are aligned at one end. Countersink the screws into the face of the gauge. Then screw this assembly into the top edge of the guide.

To use the miter gauge, position it on the infeed side of the bit with the guide flush against the edge of the table. Then butt the end of the workpiece against the fence while holding its edge flush against the gauge. With the thumbs of both hands hooked over the jig, push the workpiece and the gauge together to make the cut *(right)*.

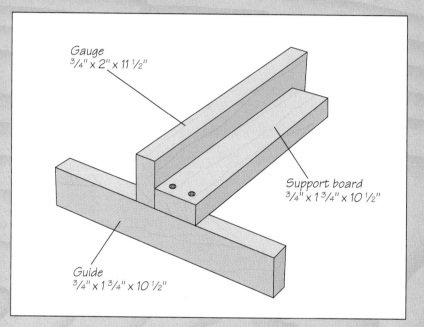

Gauge
³⁄₄" x 2" x 11 ½"

Support board
³⁄₄" x 1 ³⁄₄" x 10 ½"

Guide
³⁄₄" x 1 ³⁄₄" x 10 ½"

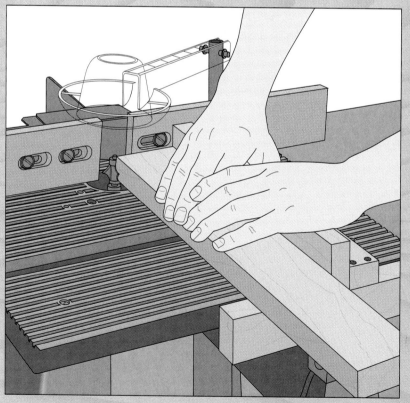

MAKING A STOPPED CUT ON A ROUTER TABLE

1 Setting up the cut
Mark a cutting line on the face of the workpiece for the end of the cut. Align the end of the stock with the cutting edge of the bit, then draw a line on a strip of masking tape to mark the position of the cutter when it is hidden by the workpiece *(right)*.

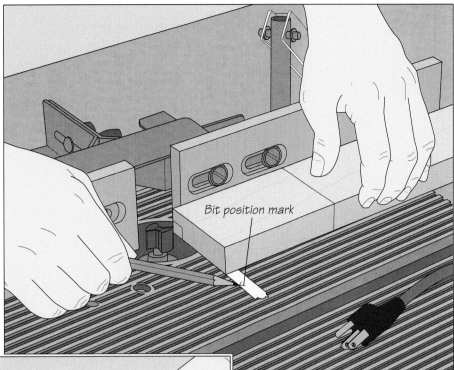

Bit position mark

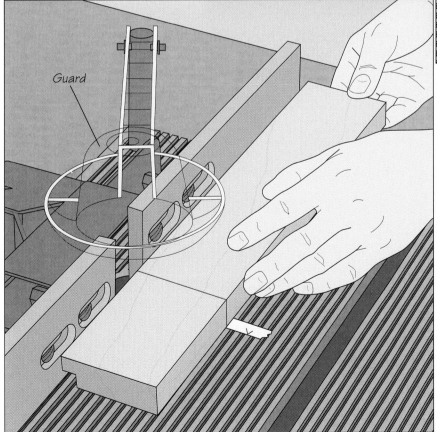

Guard

2 Feeding the stock
With the workpiece clear of the bit, position the guard and turn on the router. Press the stock flush against the fence while feeding it into the bit. Stop the cut once the cutting line of the workpiece meets the bit location mark *(left)*.

BUILD IT YOURSELF

ROUTER TABLE

Easy and inexpensive to build, the table shown below allows you to use your router as a stationary tool for shaping, molding and grooving. It features a good-sized tabletop, an adjustable fence, a storage shelf and a conveniently located On/off switch. Use ¾-inch plywood for the tabletop and the shelf, ¼-inch plywood for the support brackets, and solid lumber for the other parts. Refer to the cutting list for suggested dimensions.

Start building the table by preparing the top for the router. Bore a small hole through the center of the plywood, then outline the router base plate on its underside, aligning the collet over the hole. Use the router to plow a ¼-inch-deep recess within the outline to accept the plate. Unscrew the tool's

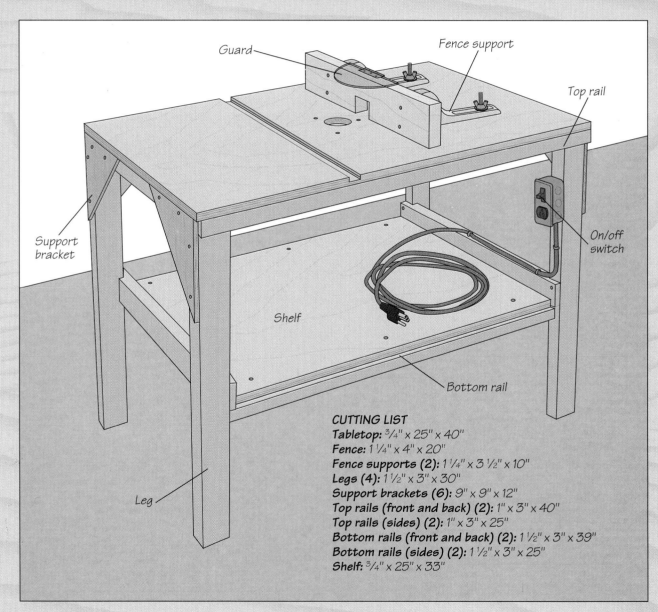

Guard

Fence support

Top rail

On/off switch

Support bracket

Shelf

Bottom rail

Leg

CUTTING LIST

Tabletop: ¾" x 25" x 40"
Fence: 1¼" x 4" x 20"
Fence supports (2): 1¼" x 3½" x 10"
Legs (4): 1½" x 3" x 30"
Support brackets (6): 9" x 9" x 12"
Top rails (front and back) (2): 1" x 3" x 40"
Top rails (sides) (2): 1" x 3" x 25"
Bottom rails (front and back) (2): 1½" x 3" x 39"
Bottom rails (sides) (2): 1½" x 3" x 25"
Shelf: ¾" x 25" x 33"

sub-base from the base plate. Remove the plate from the router and use an awl to mark its screw holes within the recess *(right, top)*. Bore holes for the screws, then fit a drill with a hole saw or spade bit wider than your largest router bit and cut a hole through the center of the top. Mount the base plate underneath the tabletop.

Use screws to assemble the parts of the table. You can either countersink the fasteners or counterbore the holes for them, and then conceal the screw heads with wood plugs.

To make the fence, cut a notch out of its bottom edge to accommodate your largest bit. Next, cut slots for bolts in the fence supports. (The slots will allow you to move the fence to set the width of cut.) Then screw on the supports. Bore holes for bolts and secure the fence supports to the tabletop with wing nuts, bolts and washers. Attach a clear plastic guard with a hinge to allow it to be raised out of the way if necessary *(right, below)*.

Fasten a combination switch-receptable to one of the legs. Wire a power cord long enough to reach a nearby outlet. When you use the table, plug in the router and leave its motor on. Use the table's switch to turn the tool on and off.

The router table can be used the same way as a commercial model *(page 91)*. To set the width of cut, loosen the wing nuts, slide the fence to the appropriate position and tighten the nuts.

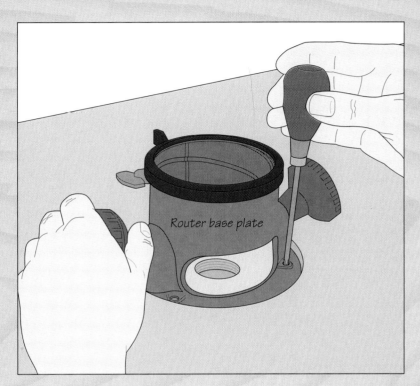

Router base plate

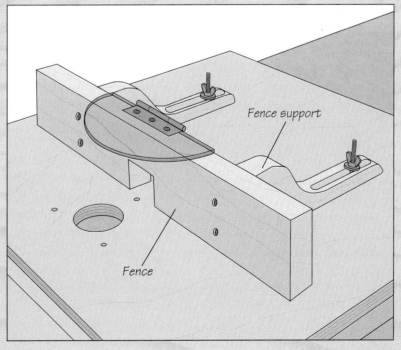

Fence support

Fence

JOINTING WITH A ROUTER TABLE

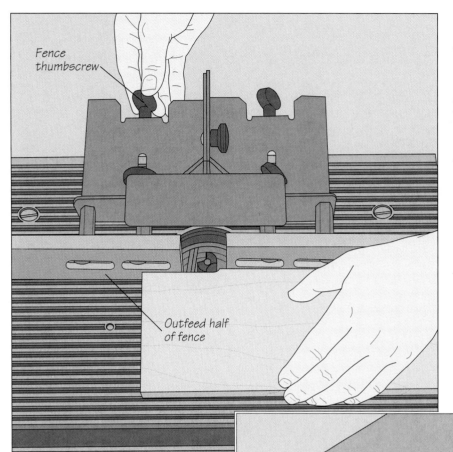

Fence
thumbscrew

Outfeed half
of fence

1 Setting up the table
Install a straight bit in the router, with a cutting edge longer than the thickness of your workpiece. To remove $\frac{1}{16}$ inch of wood from your stock—a typical amount when jointing—adjust the position of the fence for a cut of that amount. Make a test cut a few inches into a scrap board, then hold the board in place against the fence. For a router table with an adjustable split fence, loosen the fence thumbscrews *(left)* and advance the outfeed half until it butts against the cut part of the stock. Tighten the thumbscrews. If your router table has a one-piece fence, fasten a strip of veneer on the outfeed side the same width as the amount of stock removed in the test cut.

2 Jointing an edge
Butt the workpiece against the router table fence a few inches from the bit. Slowly feed the stock into the cutter *(right)*, while keeping it pressed snugly against the fence. Apply side pressure just to the outfeed side of the bit.

ROUTER JOINERY

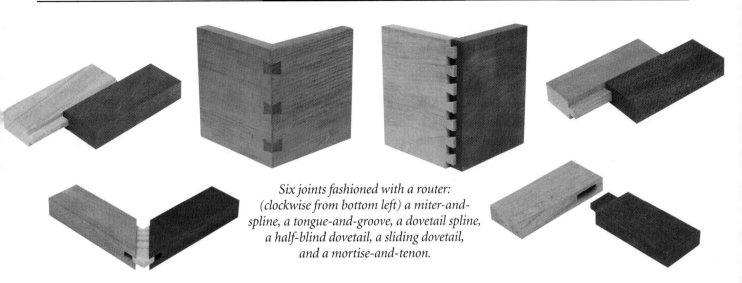

Six joints fashioned with a router: (clockwise from bottom left) a miter-and-spline, a tongue-and-groove, a dovetail spline, a half-blind dovetail, a sliding dovetail, and a mortise-and-tenon.

The router's ability to plunge into wood and cut precise grooves makes it an excellent tool for joinery. The pages that follow provide a sampling of the joints you can cut with the router. You can rough out a mortise freehand, as shown below. But many jobs are best executed with the aid of a special-purpose jig or a router table. Commercial mortise-and-tenon and dovetail jigs, for example, can help make joints quickly and with unerring accuracy.

For the long cuts required in making tongue-and-groove and sliding dovetail joints, the router table is considered by many woodworkers to be a necessity. It will give you much greater control in feeding the stock past the bit.

MAKING A MORTISE

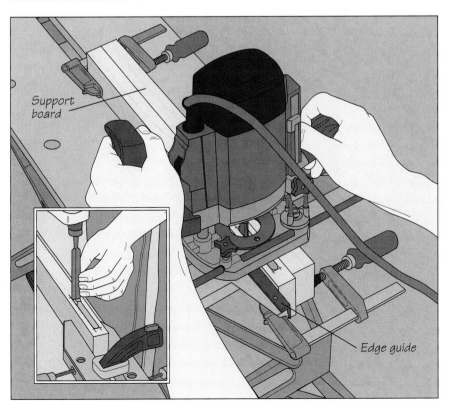

Support board

Edge guide

Routing out the cavity with a plunge router
Cut the tenon with a table saw or hand-saw and use it to outline the mortise on your stock. Secure the workpiece in a workbench, along with a board of the same width. The board will provide extra support for the router as you make the cut; make sure that the top edges of the two pieces are level. Install a mortising bit in the router the same diameter as the width of the mortise, then set the depth of cut. For a deep mortise, adjust the tool to make one or more intermediate passes. Center the bit over the outline and install a commercial edge guide on the router with the fence flush against the edge of the workpiece. Holding the tool firmly, plunge the bit into the stock at one end of the outline, then feed the cutter to the other end *(left)*. Secure the workpiece in handscrews as shown in the inset and square the corners of the mortise with a chisel, keeping the blade square to the workpiece and the bevel facing the waste.

ROUTING WITH A MORTISE-AND-TENON JIG

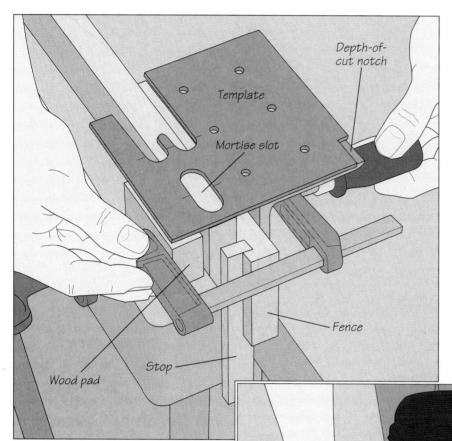

1 Setting up the jig
Assemble a commercial mortise-and-tenon jig following the manufacturer's instructions. The model shown allows you to cut both the mortise and tenon with the same setup. To prepare the jig to make the cut, fit the stop in the fence at the mortise-end of the device. Secure the jig in a vise, then clamp the workpiece to it with the end of the board butted against the stop and the edge flush against the template as shown. Protect the stock with wood pads *(left)*. Install the bit supplied with the template in your router. To set the cutting depth, hold the tool's base plate against the edge of the template and align the tip of the bit with the bottom of the depth-of-cut notch.

Depth-of-cut notch

Template

Mortise slot

Fence

Wood pad

Stop

2 Routing the mortise with a plunge router
Hold the router flat on the jig template with the bit centered over one end of the mortise slot. Plunge the bit into the stock *(right)*, then feed the tool along the template to the other end of the slot to finish the cut. Make sure you keep the bit pilot against the inside edges of the slot throughout the operation. (Router sub-base removed for clarity.) Remove the workpiece from the jig and the jig from the vise.

3 Adjusting the jig for the tenon

Fit the stop in the slot in the fence at the the opposite end of the jig. Unscrew the template and shift it toward the tenon-end slots so that one of the alignment pins on the jig body is exposed as shown. Refasten the template, then secure the jig and the tenon workpiece in the vise; position the board so that its edge butts against the stop and its end rests against the template *(right)*.

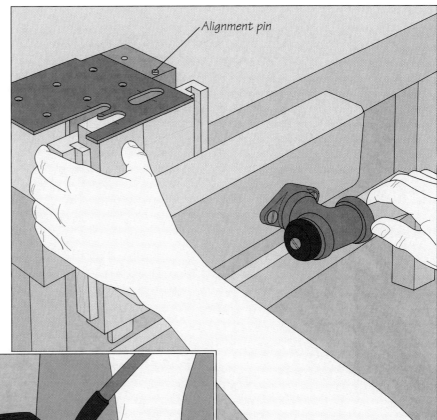

Alignment pin

4 Routing the tenon

The tenon is cut in two passes. Make the first cut the same way you routed the mortise in step 2, riding the pilot along the inside edges of the tenon-end slots *(left)*. Then turn off the router and unscrew the template from the jig body. Turn the template over end-for-end and refasten it to the jig, keeping the same alignment pin exposed as for the first pass, then finish routing the tenon.

MAKING A TONGUE-AND-GROOVE JOINT

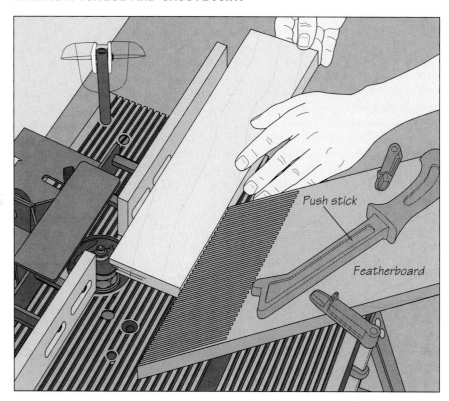

Push stick

Featherboard

1 Cutting the groove
Install an appropriate-sized three-wing slotting cutter in the router, then mount the tool in a table. Adjust the fence to make the width of cut equal to the bit diameter *(page 91)*. To set the cutting depth, place the workpiece flat on the table and center the bit on the edge of the stock. For added stability, clamp one featherboard to the table, and a second one to the fence above the bit. (In the illustrations on this page, the upper featherboard is removed for clarity.) With the stock clear of the bit, turn on the router and slowly feed the workpiece into the cutter *(left)*. Finish the pass with a push stick.

2 Cutting the tongue
Remove the router from the table, insert a straight-cutting bit and remount the tool. Adjust the fence to make the width of cut equal to the depth of the groove you have already cut. The cutting depth should equal the amount of stock remaining on either side of the groove. Feed the workpiece into the cutter as in step 1.

CUTTING A HALF-BLIND DOVETAIL JOINT

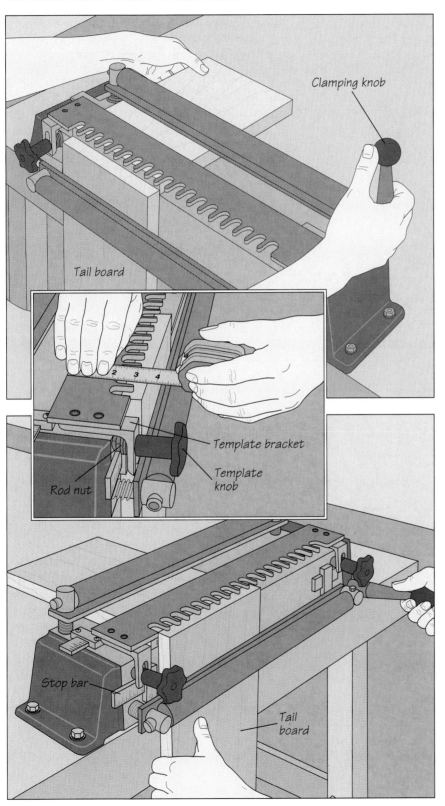

Clamping knob

Tail board

Template bracket

Template knob

Rod nut

Stop bar

Tail board

1 Securing the boards in the jig
Set up a router jig for cutting dovetails following the manufacturer's instructions. The model shown allows you to rout the pins and tails of a half-blind dovetail joint with a single setup. To get the jig ready, slide the two stop bars on the left-hand side of the jig body out of the way by loosening the setscrews and hex nuts holding them in place. Loosen the template knobs and remove the pattern. Install both boards inside face out in the jig: the tail board against the front of the jig body with its end projecting ¼ inch above the body, and the pin board flat on the jig butted against the tail board. Position the template on the workpieces leaving a gap of $^{19}/_{32}$ inch between the end of the pin board and the bottom of the template slots *(inset)*. Turn the rod nuts for fine adjustment of the template's position, then tighten the template knobs to secure the pattern in place. To position the stock for the cut, mark a line $^{3}/_{16}$ inch from the left-hand edge of the pin board. Slide the board over to align the mark with the left-hand edge of the first template slot. Use the clamping knob to secure the board in position *(left, top)*. Then move the tail board so that its left-hand edge is $^{7}/_{16}$ inch from the edge of the pin board *(left, bottom)*. Butt the two stop bars against the boards and fix them in place.

2 Routing the dovetails

To prepare your router to cut ½-inch dovetails, install a ⅝-inch template guide on the tool *(page 88)*. Insert a ½-inch dovetail bit and set the cutting depth to $^{21}/_{32}$ inch. Rout the pins and tails in two passes. Start the first pass at the right-hand edge of the tail board; cut in a straight line to its left-hand edge, running the template guide along the tips of the slots. This will remove about half of the waste wood from the tail board. Then rout back in the opposite direction, following the contours of the template. Move in and out of the slots, keeping the guide flush against the edges of the fingers at all times. Continue to the right-hand edge of the boards *(right)*. This pass will cut the pins and remove the remaining waste from the tail board.

ROUTING A MITER-SPLINE JOINT

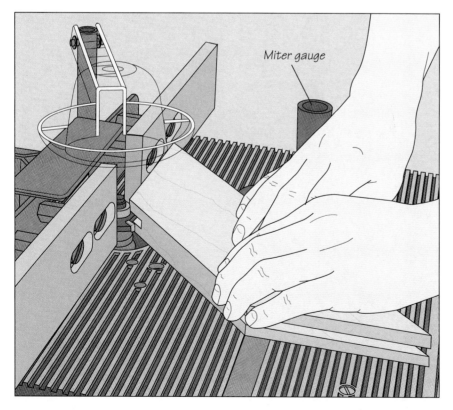

Miter gauge

Cutting the grooves

Make 45° miter cuts at both ends of the workpiece. Then mount your router in a table with a three-wing slotting cutter and set the width and depth of cut as you would to cut the groove for a tongue-and-groove joint *(page 100)*. Feed the stock into the bit with a miter gauge, holding the edge of the board flush against the gauge and one mitered end flat along the fence. Repeat to cut the groove in the other board end *(left)*. Cut a spline for each joint, making each one twice as wide as the groove depth, less ¹⁄₁₆ inch for clearance. For maximum strength, use plywood or solid wood cut with the grain of the splines running across their width, rather than along their length.

MAKING A SLIDING DOVETAIL JOINT

1 Cutting a preliminary straight groove
Cut a dovetail groove in two passes, first with a straight-cutting bit to remove most of the waste wood, and then with a dovetail bit to complete the groove. For the first pass, install a straight-cutting bit in your router, then mount the tool in a table. Set the cutting depth, then position the fence for the width of cut by centering an edge of the workpiece over the bit and butting the fence against the face of the stock. Clamp a featherboard to the table to secure the workpiece during the cut. Feed the stock into the bit with both hands, making sure you keep the workpiece flush against the fence *(right)*. Complete the pass with a push stick, then remove the router from the table.

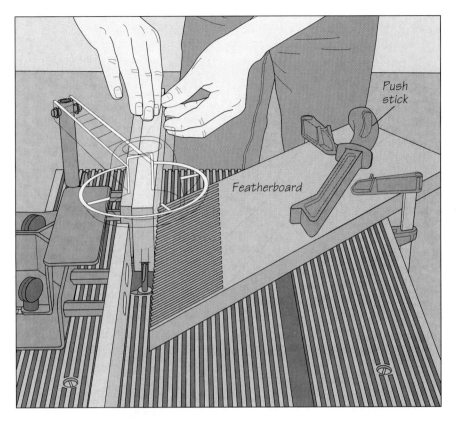

Push stick

Featherboard

2 Making the dovetail groove
For the second pass, install a dovetail bit in the router. Feed the workpiece into the bit the same way you cut the straight groove, taking care to press the edge of the stock flat against the table throughout the operation *(left)*.

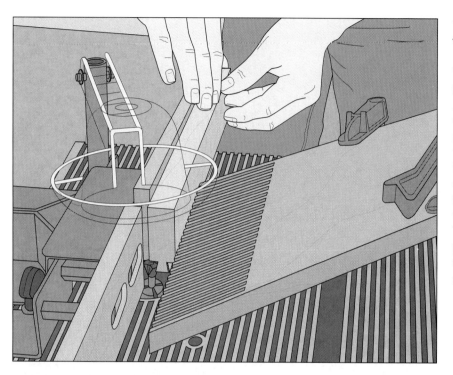

3 Routing the matching dovetail slide

With the dovetail bit still in the router, lower the cutting depth slightly to make the slide shorter than the depth of the groove; this will improve the fit of the joint. Move the fence toward the bit until exactly half the diameter of the cutter projects beyond the fence, then shift the featherboard accordingly. Cut the slide in two passes, removing the waste from each side at a time. Make the first pass the same way you cut the groove, running the face of the workpiece along the fence. To finish cutting the slide, turn the workpiece around and make the second pass with the opposite face of the stock flush against the fence *(left)*.

CUTTING A DOVETAIL SPLINE JOINT

1 Preparing the jig

To cut perfectly matching grooves into the ends of two boards for a dovetail spline joint, use the jig shown at right, shop-built from ¾-inch plywood. Refer to the illustration for suggested dimensions. Before assembling the jig, cut the oval-shaped slot in the middle of the base with a saber saw; the hole should be large enough to accommodate the router bit you will use to cut the grooves. Then make 45° bevels at the top ends of the arms and the bottom ends of the support brackets. Fasten the arms to the base and the support brackets to both the base and the arms with screws and glue. Make sure that the arms are perfectly perpendicular to each other; check that the joint between them is centered under the slot. Install a dovetail bit in your router, secure the jig in a vise, then cut a channel through the slot across the mitered ends of the arms. Turn off the tool and, with the bit still in the channel, butt a board as an edge guide against the tool's base plate, then screw it to the jig base *(right)*.

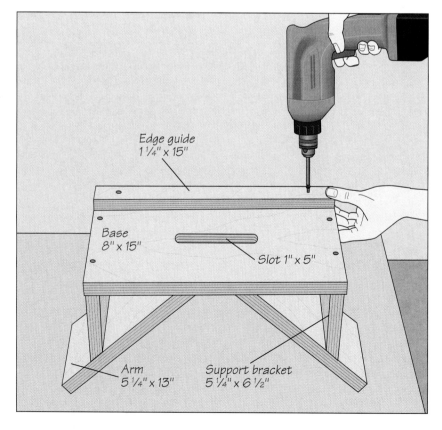

Edge guide
1 ¼" x 15"

Base
8" x 15"

Slot 1" x 5"

Arm
5 ¼" x 13"

Support bracket
5 ¼" x 6 ½"

2 Routing the grooves

Make 45° bevel cuts at the mating ends of both workpieces, then mark cutting lines for the grooves. Position the workpieces in the jig under the arms, with their beveled ends butted against each other under the channel you routed in step 1. Align the cutting lines on the boards with the edges of the channel, then secure them in place with a clamp. To rout the grooves, repeat the cut you made to rout the channel, feeding the bit through the ends of both workpieces. Be sure to keep the router flat on the jig base as you make the cut *(right)*.

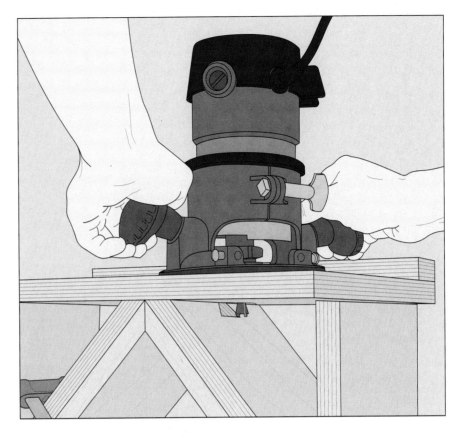

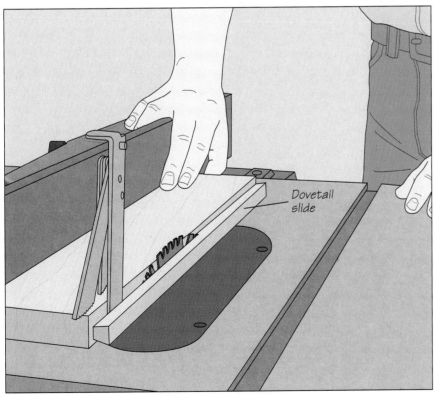

Dovetail slide

3 Making the dovetail splines

You will need splines to fit into the grooves cut in step 2. To make enough splines for several joints, rout a dovetail slide as you would for a sliding dovetail joint *(page 104)*, using the same dovetail bit that cut the grooves. Then cut the slide from the edge of the board on a table saw. Feed the stock with your right hand as shown, making sure that your fingers are not in line with the blade. **(Caution: Blade guard removed for clarity.)** Cut the slide into individual splines. Then clamp the mating boards to a work surface, spread some glue in the grooves and on the splines and drive them in place with a mallet. Once the glue has dried, cut and sand the ends of the splines flush with the boards.

PLATE JOINER

Mounted in a bench top stand, the plate joiner becomes a stationary tool, keeping your hands free to feed stock into the cutter for a series of identical cuts.

Popular with European cabinetmakers since the 1950s, plate joiners are still a novelty to many North American woodworkers. This is destined to change, for although a plate joiner is usually designed to perform only one task—joining two boards—it does that job very quickly and well. The tool features a retractable, spring-mounted blade that cuts slots in mating workpieces. Glue is applied to the slots and an oval-shaped biscuit of compressed beech is inserted in each one. The wooden wafers rapidly absorb the adhesive and swell, making a solid joint.

As this section of the book shows, plate joinery is a simple way to fasten boards together edge-to-edge *(page 112)* or join carcase panels at the corners *(page 114)*, whether the ends are square or beveled. It is also a quick method for installing shelves in a carcase *(page 116)*.

Compared to cutting a dovetail or mortise-and-tenon joint, operating a plate joiner is relatively simple. The tool's faceplate is butted against the workpiece, guidelines on the tool are aligned with cutting marks on the stock, and the motor housing is then pushed forward, plunging the blade into the wood. The only accessories you will need are an assortment of biscuits and a

supply of white or yellow glue. (Plate joiners are also known as biscuit joiners because of the central role the wood biscuits play in the joinery method.) Three different sizes of wafers are available, depending on the thickness of the stock that you are joining.

Plate joiners are relatively safe to use; the blade projects from the tool only while it is cutting. They are also forgiving tools. Because the slots are cut slightly larger than the biscuits, a groove can be off-center by as much as $1/16$ inch without affecting the alignment of a joint. The same error in a dovetail joint would add another piece of wood to your scrap pile.

Most plate joiners are equipped to cut slots at either 90° or 45° to the top face of the stock. While these angles will cover most joints you are likely to design, you should consider buying a joiner with an adjustable fence. It will enable you to cut a slot at any angle from 0° to 90°.

Possibly in response to the impression that plate joiners are strictly one-dimensional tools, most manufacturers now offer wood-trimming blades as an option. Some have even designed their joiners to serve as mini-power saws, which can comfortably trim a plywood panel or cut grooves.

With a spray of sawdust, a plate joiner cuts a semicircular slot in a tapered leg. A wood biscuit and glue will be added to the cut and then fitted into a mating slot in a rail. The resulting joint will be as strong as a mortise-and-tenon—and far easier to make.

ANATOMY OF A PLATE JOINER

Though all plate joiners cut slots in essentially the same way, their designs differ. Most joiners, like the one shown opposite, have motors mounted in line with the cutter wheel; to cut a slot the housing is pushed forward so the blade protrudes through its opening and plunges into the stock. An alternate design features a motor and a handle mounted at an angle to the cutter wheel—either with the motor completely upright or, as in the joiner illustrated in the photo *(below, right)*, at a 45° angle to the blade. In this case, the handle must be pivoted forward to cut a biscuit slot. A third, less-common option is the stationary plate joiner *(below, left)*, a useful addition for a shop that depends heavily on plate joinery.

All joiners have a depth-of-cut adjustment for each of the three biscuit sizes. Some models offer additional settings to cut slots for accessories such as hinges and knockdown fittings. Other desirable features to look for when buying a tool include an adjustable fence for cutting slots in beveled surfaces, a fixed-angle fence that references the cutter wheel to the top face of a workpiece, and a dust collection bag.

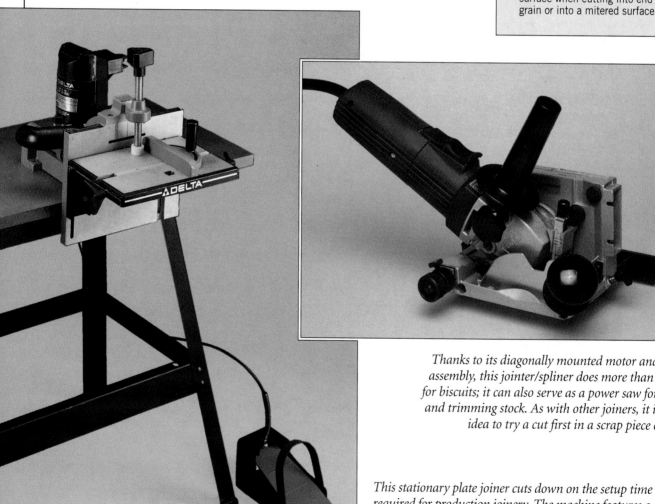

Thanks to its diagonally mounted motor and handle assembly, this jointer/spliner does more than cut slots for biscuits; it can also serve as a power saw for cutting and trimming stock. As with other joiners, it is a good idea to try a cut first in a scrap piece of wood.

This stationary plate joiner cuts down on the setup time required for production joinery. The machine features a metal fence and miter gauge to guide stock across its table when cutting grooves, a hold-down clamp to secure a workpiece for plate joining, and a foot switch.

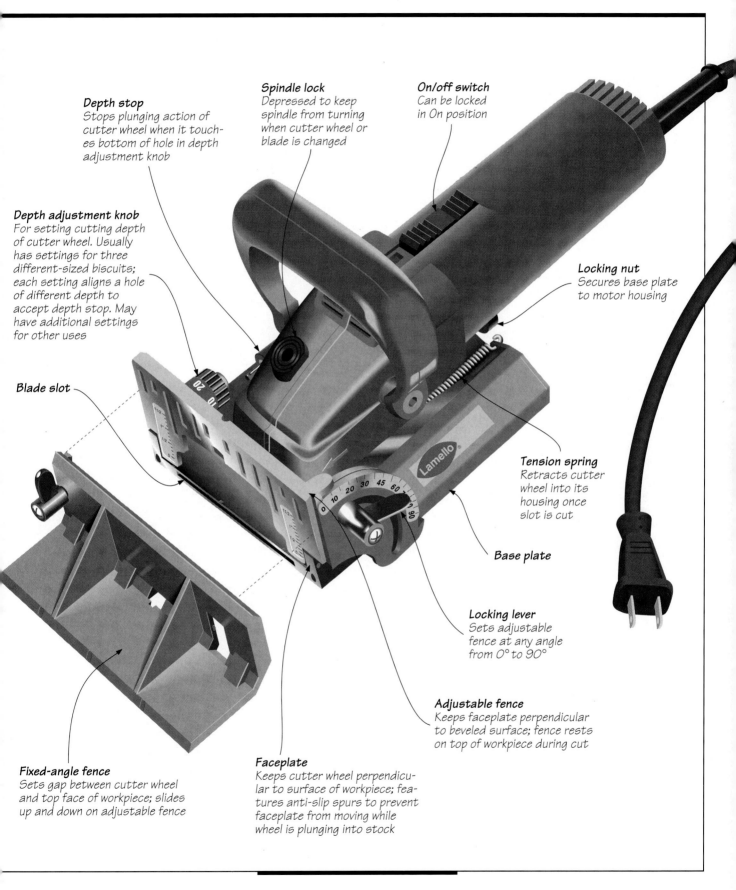

Depth stop
Stops plunging action of cutter wheel when it touches bottom of hole in depth adjustment knob

Spindle lock
Depressed to keep spindle from turning when cutter wheel or blade is changed

On/off switch
Can be locked in On position

Depth adjustment knob
For setting cutting depth of cutter wheel. Usually has settings for three different-sized biscuits; each setting aligns a hole of different depth to accept depth stop. May have additional settings for other uses

Locking nut
Secures base plate to motor housing

Blade slot

Tension spring
Retracts cutter wheel into its housing once slot is cut

Base plate

Locking lever
Sets adjustable fence at any angle from 0° to 90°

Adjustable fence
Keeps faceplate perpendicular to beveled surface; fence rests on top of workpiece during cut

Fixed-angle fence
Sets gap between cutter wheel and top face of workpiece; slides up and down on adjustable fence

Faceplate
Keeps cutter wheel perpendicular to surface of workpiece; features anti-slip spurs to prevent faceplate from moving while wheel is plunging into stock

PLATE JOINER ACCESSORIES

The most important accessories for a plate joiner are the biscuits used to join boards or panels. Wood biscuits come in three sizes *(photo, opposite)*; as a general rule, the size of the biscuit increases with the thickness of the stock being joined.

Beech biscuits are much stronger than they appear. The wooden wafers are cut with the grain running diagonal to their edges, making them virtually impossible to snap down the middle. Their surfaces also feature an embossed crosshatch pattern. This helps glue adhere to the biscuits, which swell as they absorb the adhesive.

Other types of biscuits are also available. There are plastic types that help to hold a joint together when clamping the pieces is difficult or impractical. And there are metal knockdown fittings that mesh together, so as to allow furniture to be assembled without glue, and then be taken apart again. These specialty biscuits are only available in the large size.

The standard cutter wheel supplied with some plate joiners can be exchanged for a wood-trimming or grooving blade, transforming the joiner into a power saw that can make quick work of cutting grooves for splines or trimming thin plywood panels to width. Although the teeth on the cutter wheel should hold a sharp cutting edge through years of use, they may need to be sharpened from time to time.

INSTALLING A WOOD-TRIMMING BLADE

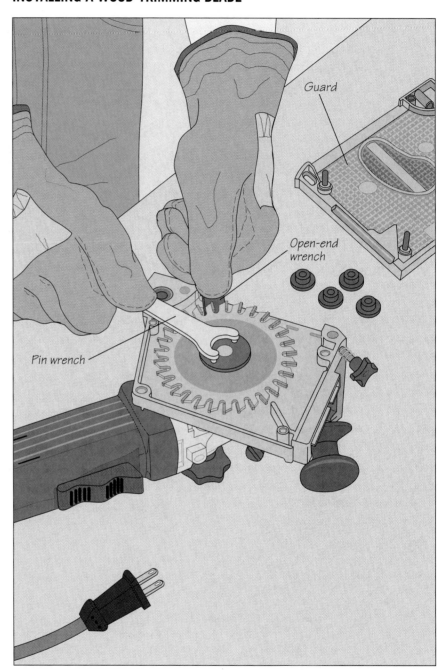

Changing a blade
Unscrew the nuts holding the guard in place and set it aside. Fit the open-end wrench supplied with the tool around the inner clamp washer under the cutter wheel. Then loosen the outer clamp washer by turning it clockwise with the pin wrench. Wear leather gloves to protect your hands in case one of the wrenches slips. Remove the washer and the cutter wheel from the spindle, then install the wood-trimming blade with its teeth pointing in a clockwise direction. Retighten the outer clamp washer *(above)* and screw the guard back in place.

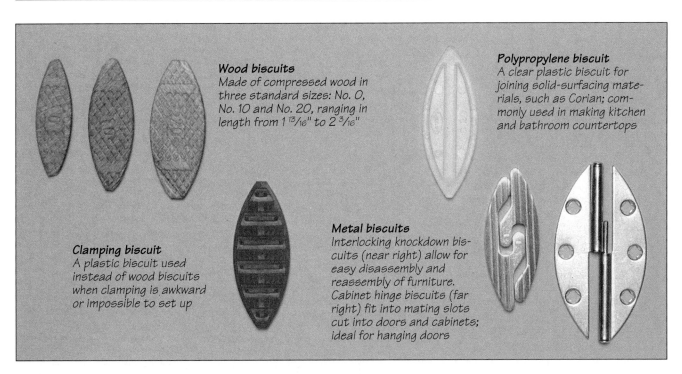

Wood biscuits
Made of compressed wood in three standard sizes: No. 0, No. 10 and No. 20, ranging in length from 1 $^{13}/_{16}$" to 2 $^{3}/_{16}$"

Polypropylene biscuit
A clear plastic biscuit for joining solid-surfacing materials, such as Corian; commonly used in making kitchen and bathroom countertops

Clamping biscuit
A plastic biscuit used instead of wood biscuits when clamping is awkward or impossible to set up

Metal biscuits
Interlocking knockdown biscuits (near right) allow for easy disassembly and reassembly of furniture. Cabinet hinge biscuits (far right) fit into mating slots cut into doors and cabinets; ideal for hanging doors

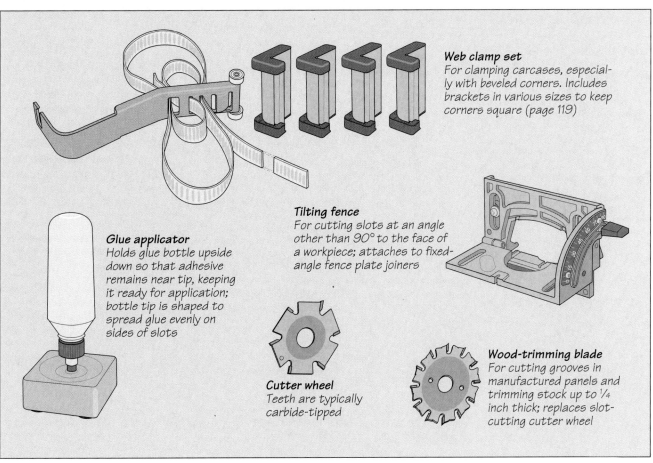

Web clamp set
For clamping carcases, especially with beveled corners. Includes brackets in various sizes to keep corners square (page 119)

Glue applicator
Holds glue bottle upside down so that adhesive remains near tip, keeping it ready for application; bottle tip is shaped to spread glue evenly on sides of slots

Tilting fence
For cutting slots at an angle other than 90° to the face of a workpiece; attaches to fixed-angle fence plate joiners

Cutter wheel
Teeth are typically carbide-tipped

Wood-trimming blade
For cutting grooves in manufactured panels and trimming stock up to 1/4 inch thick; replaces slot-cutting cutter wheel

PLATE JOINERY

Although not decorative like dovetails, plate joints are a quick method of joining carcase panels together, edge gluing boards into panels, or adding shelves to a carcase. As strong and durable as mortise-and-tenon joints, they are also ideal for straightening warped boards when edge gluing them to make a broad surface like a tabletop.

The biscuit size you select for a project will depend on the thickness of your stock. Use No. 0 biscuits for wood ¼ to ½ inch thick, No. 10s for ½- to ¾-inch-thick stock, and No. 20s for thicker boards. For even larger stock, you can provide additional reinforcement by cutting parallel slots for two biscuits *(page 117)*.

Set the depth of cut on a joiner according to the biscuit size you are using. There are no prescribed rules for spacing biscuits, but the closer you place them, the stronger the joint. As a rule of thumb, locate them 4 to 8 inches apart. Biscuits

are effective because they absorb moisture and swell, but humidity will also make them expand, so store them in sealed plastic bags in a dry location.

Plate joints do not demand the same precision involved in other methods of joinery. For example, the slots need not be centered exactly in a board's edge or end. However, avoid making the slots too close to a board face. Although it may not

show through initially, a biscuit inserted within ¼ inch of a face may produce a dimple on the surface after the stock is sanded. This unsightly effect is known as "biscuit pucker."

Always dry assemble a joint to test its fit. Plate joints are virtually impossible to adjust after gluing. The biscuits swell so quickly that trying to remove one from a slot—even only minutes after applying the glue—is difficult. The thin wooden wafers or the sides of the slots may break instead.

A butt joint with a difference: Once glue is added to the slots in the boards, the biscuit will swell, filling the slots and creating a solid, long-lasting joint.

EDGE GLUING BOARDS

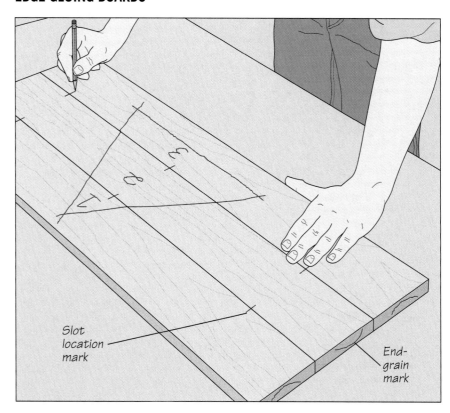

Slot location mark

End-grain mark

1 Marking the location of the slots
Mark the end grain orientation of the boards, then arrange the stock to produce a pattern that is visually interesting. To minimize cupping on the finished surface, make sure that the end grain of adjacent boards runs in opposite directions. Draw a triangle across the face of the stock once you have a satisfactory arrangement; this will help you quickly realign the boards when necessary. Mark center lines for the slots across the seams between adjacent boards. Start at least 2 inches in from each end and add a mark every 4 to 8 inches.

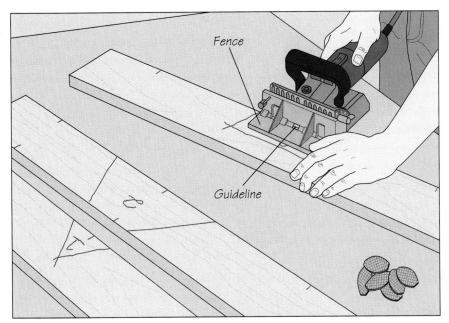

Fence

Guideline

2 Cutting the slots
Resting the fence on top of the stock, align the guideline on the faceplate with a slot location mark. Switch on the tool and push it into the board to cut the groove *(left)*. Repeat the procedure at the other locations. With thin stock, the base plate may touch the work surface, shifting the alignment of the slots. To prevent this, position the workpiece at the table's edge so the base plate does not contact the tabletop.

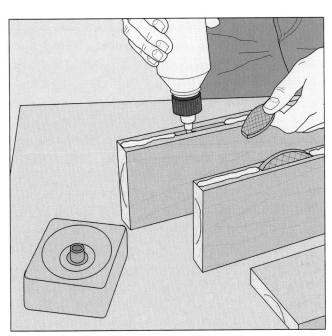

Notched wood block

3 Inserting the biscuits
Once all the slots have been cut, leave the last board face down and stand the others on edge with the slots facing up. Squeeze a bead of glue into the slots and along the edges of the boards, inserting biscuits as you go *(above)*. The glue bottle shown here automatically applies adhesive evenly on the sides of the slots; if you are using a standard bottle, spread the glue with a thin wooden stick. Assemble the boards quickly to prevent the biscuits from expanding prematurely.

4 Gluing up the boards
Fit the boards together, making sure that the sides of the triangle are aligned. Lay the boards on bar clamps—one for each 24- to 36-inch interval. To keep the clamps from moving, place them in notched wood blocks. Protect the stock with wood pads, then tighten the clamps just enough to close the joints. Place a third clamp across the top, centering it between the other two. Continue tightening all the clamps until glue squeezes out of the joints.

JOINING CARCASE CORNERS

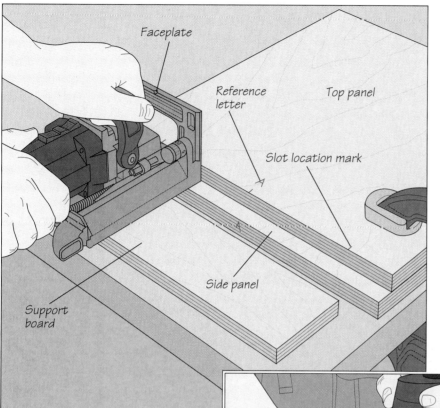

Faceplate

Reference letter

Top panel

Slot location mark

Side panel

Support board

1 Cutting slots in the top panel
Lay one of the side panels outside-face down on a work surface and set the top piece outside-face up on top of it, adding reference letters to identify the corners. Set back the edge of the top panel by an amount equal to the thickness of the stock, then clamp the two pieces in place. Set a support board the same thickness as the stock in front of the workpieces, then mark slot location lines on the top panel. This setup will allow you to cut all the grooves for one corner of the carcase without moving the panels. Resting the plate joiner on the support board, align the guideline on the faceplate with a slot location mark on the stock. Hold the joiner with both hands and make the cut *(left)*. Repeat the process at the other marks.

2 Cutting slots in the side panel
Once all the grooves have been cut in the top panel, align the guideline in the center of the tool's base plate with a slot mark *(right)*. Cut all the grooves in the side panel, then repeat the clamping and cutting procedure on the other corners of the carcase.

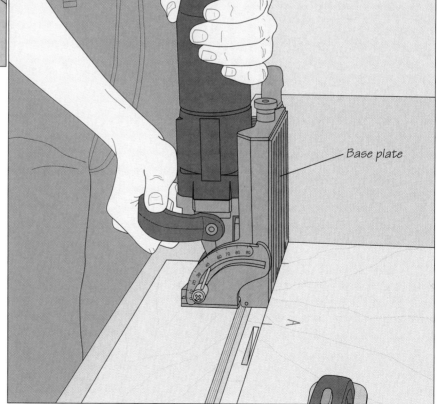

Base plate

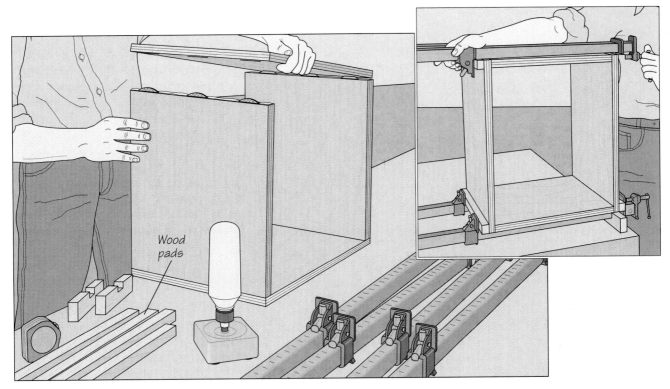

Wood pads

3 Gluing up the carcase

Set the side panels on the work surface outside face down. Apply glue and insert biscuits into their slots as for edge gluing boards *(page 113)*. On the top and bottom panels, squeeze a bead of glue into each slot and along the edges between the slots. Assemble the carcase, fitting the top and bottom panels onto one side and then adding the other side *(above)*. Install two bar clamps across the top and bottom, protecting the workpieces with wood pads. Tighten the clamps a little at a time *(inset)* until glue starts to squeeze out of the joints. To check whether the carcase is square, measure the diagonals between opposite corners immediately after tightening the clamps. The results should be the same. If not, install a fifth clamp across the longer diagonal and tighten it until the carcase is square.

SHOP TIP

Wooden gauge blocks

To set your plate joiner's fence so that slots will be cut precisely in the center of board edges, make a series of gauge blocks. The thickness of each block should be the distance between the base plate and the middle of the cutter wheel plus one-half the thickness of the workpiece. To use a gauge block, place the joiner flat on a work surface and adjust the fence until it rests on the appropriate-sized block.

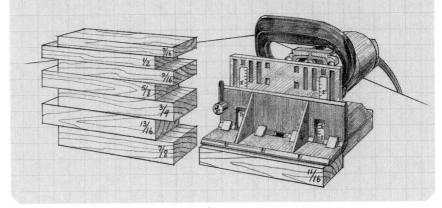

ADDING A SHELF TO A CARCASE

Shelf

Slot location mark

Reference letter

Side panel

Slots for corner joint

1 Marking the slot locations
Cut slots for the corner joints *(page 114)*, then lay the side panel on the work surface, outside-face down. Draw slot location marks at both ends of the shelf. Decide where you want the shelf and draw a line on the side panel with a carpenter's square to mark its position *(left)*. Draw a corresponding line on the other side panel, making sure that the ends of the two pieces are aligned so the opposite ends of the shelf will be perfectly level. To help you keep track of how the parts join together, use matching reference letters.

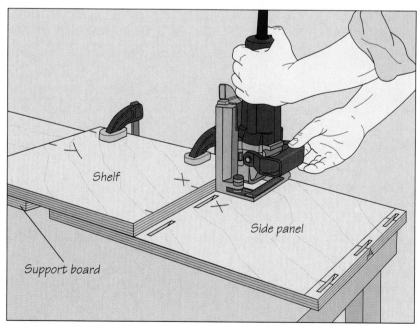

Shelf

Side panel

Support board

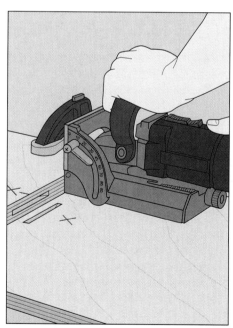

2 Cutting the slots
Position the shelf atop one side panel, its edge aligned with the reference line. Place a support board the same thickness as the panel under the shelf to keep it level, then clamp the workpieces in position. To cut the slots in the panel, butt the tool's base plate against the shelf, aligning the guideline in the center of the plate with the shelf's slot location marks *(above, left)*. To cut the slots in the shelf, line up the guide line on the faceplace with each of the marks *(above, right)*. Reposition the shelf with its uncut end on the reference line of the other side panel, and repeat the slot-cutting procedure.

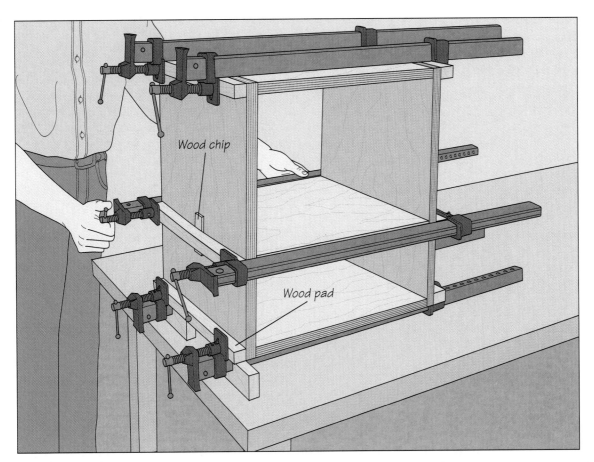

Wood chip

Wood pad

3 Gluing up the carcase
Apply glue and add biscuits to the shelf and corner joints following the procedure for gluing a carcase without a shelf *(page 115)*. Assemble the carcase with the shelf in place and clamp it at top and bottom. Close the shelf joints with bar clamps at front and back, protecting the side panels with wood pads; place a ¼-inch-thick wood chip under each pad to focus some of the pressure midway between the edges of the shelf. Tighten the clamps a little at a time until a trace of glue squeezes out of the joints.

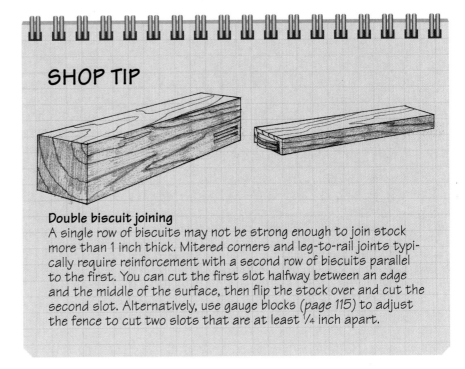

SHOP TIP

Double biscuit joining
A single row of biscuits may not be strong enough to join stock more than 1 inch thick. Mitered corners and leg-to-rail joints typically require reinforcement with a second row of biscuits parallel to the first. You can cut the first slot halfway between an edge and the middle of the surface, then flip the stock over and cut the second slot. Alternatively, use gauge blocks *(page 115)* to adjust the fence to cut two slots that are at least ¼ inch apart.

JOINING BEVELED CORNERS

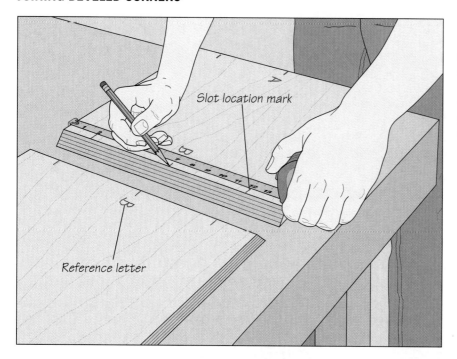

Slot location mark

Reference letter

1 Marking the location of the slots
Place two adjacent panels on a work surface, inside-faces up. Use a tape measure and pencil to mark slot locations on both pieces *(left)*. Start about 2 inches in from the edges, spacing the lines at 4- to 8-inch intervals. Repeat the procedure at the other three corners of the carcase.

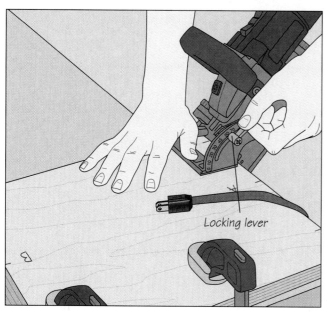

Locking lever

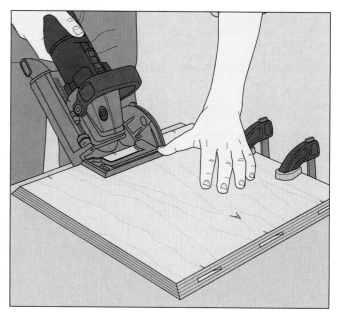

2 Cutting the slots
Clamp a panel to a work surface with one of its beveled ends projecting off the edge of the table. Butt the plate joiner's faceplate against the end and loosen the locking lever to release the adjustable fence. Swivel the fence downward against the face of the panel, then lock it in place while the faceplate is perfectly flush against the bevel *(above, left)*. If your joiner does not have an adjustable fence, use an angled block instead *(page 119)*. Align the guideline on the faceplate with a slot location and plunge the cutter into the stock *(above, right)*. Use the same technique to cut all the remaining slots.

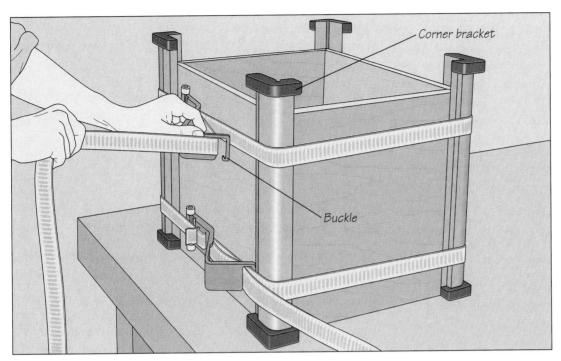

Corner bracket

Buckle

3 Gluing up the carcase
Apply glue and insert biscuits in the slots the same way you would for a carcase without beveled corners *(page 115)*. To prevent the beveled edges from slipping out of alignment as the adhesive is drying, secure the carcase with web clamps. To use the type shown here, set the carcase on its back on a work surface and fit the corner brackets in place. The brackets will help to distribute pressure evenly along the length of the joint. Wrap straps around the unit and tighten them with the buckles before locking them in place *(above)*.

SHOP TIP

An angled block for beveled surfaces
You can use your plate joiner to cut slots into beveled surfaces even if it is not equipped with an adjustable fence. Cut a wood block to the same length and width as your tool's fixed-angle fence, then cut a bevel on the block with the same angle as that of the workpiece. Screw the block to the fence with the cut edge facing down. Cut the slots as you would with an adjustable fence *(page 118)*, butting the block against the face of the workpiece and the faceplate against the beveled surface.

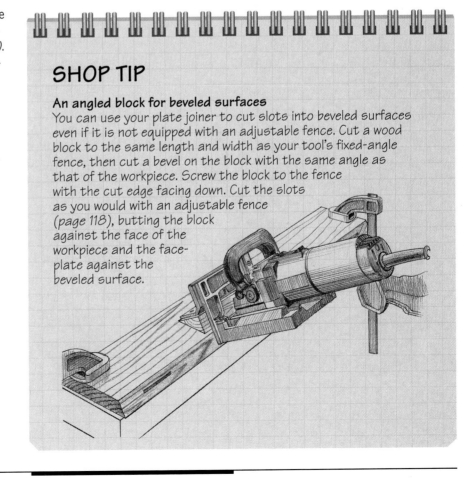

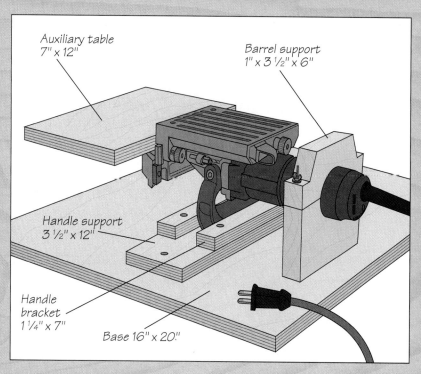

Auxiliary table
7" x 12"

Barrel support
1" x 3 ½" x 6"

Handle support
3 ½" x 12"

Handle
bracket
1 ¼" x 7"

Base 16" x 20."

Stop block

PLATE JOINER STAND

To reduce the setup time needed to cut slots in a series of workpieces, mount your plate joiner in a shop-made stand like the one shown at left. Build the jig from ¾-inch plywood, except for the barrel support, which should be solid wood. Refer to the illustration for suggested dimensions.

Screw the handle support to the base, then attach the handle brackets, spacing them to fit your tool. With the plate joiner resting upside down on the handle support, butt the barrel support against the motor housing and trace the outline of the barrel on the stock. Cut or bore a hole for the barrel, then cut the support in two across its width, through the center of the hole. Screw the bottom part to the base and fit the other half on top. Bore holes for hanger bolts through the top on each side of the opening, then drive the hanger bolts into the bottom of the support. For quick installation and removal of the tool, use wing nuts to hold the two halves together.

Screw the auxiliary table to the fixed-angle fence of the joiner. (It may be necessary to drill holes in the fence for the screws.)

To use the stand, secure the joiner in it, then clamp the base to a work surface. Set the fence at the correct height and, for repeat cuts, clamp stop blocks to the auxiliary table to center the workpiece on the cutter wheel. To cut a slot, put the workpiece flat on the table and butted against the joiner's faceplate, then turn on the tool and push the stock and the table toward the cutter (left, below).

THE PLATE JOINER AS GROOVER AND TRIMMER

Some plate joiners are designed to do more than cut slots for biscuits. The model shown on this page—dubbed a jointer/spliner by its manufacturer—can also serve as a small circular saw. Equipped with the appropriate blade, it can make an accurate crosscut or rip through a ¼-inch plywood panel, or mill a groove from one end of a workpiece to the other.

The cutter wheels that joiners normally use have 6 to 12 teeth. To ensure smooth cuts, the wood-trimming blade *(page 110)* available for the jointer/spliner has more than double that number.

Always attach an edge guide to the base plate to keep the tool cutting in a straight line. And remember to always push the tool, never pull it.

Equipped with a wood-trimming blade and an edge guide, this plate joiner makes quick work of cutting a groove in a hardwood board.

TRIMMING A PANEL

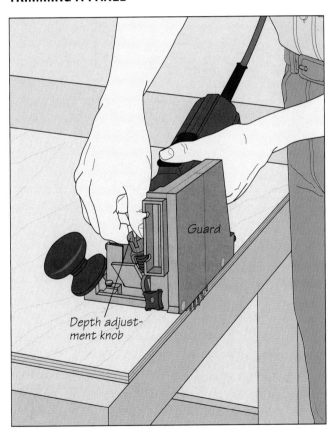

1 Setting the cutting depth
Clamp down the panel so that its edge extends beyond the work surface. Unscrew the pins that are normally fixed to the bottom of the guard to prevent them from gouging your stock. Set the joiner on the workpiece, tilt the barrel forward to lower the blade, and butt the blade against the edge of the stock. Turn the depth adjustment knob on the opposite side of the guard until the bottom teeth are about ¼ inch below the stock.

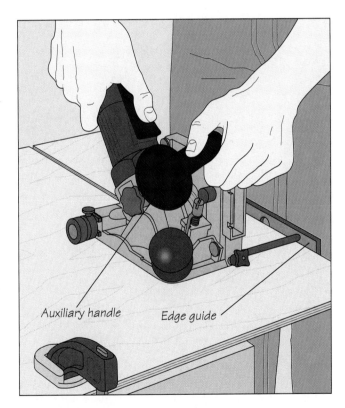

2 Making a crosscut
Install the joiner's auxiliary handle, then attach a commercial edge guide; the type shown features rods that fit into the tool's base plate. Align the blade with the cutting line, butt the fence of the guide against the end of the panel, and lock the guide in place. Clamp the workpiece with the cutting line beyond the edge of the work surface. Holding the joiner by the barrel and the auxiliary handle, turn it on. Tilt the blade down and push it into the panel, keeping the edge guide fence flush against the stock as you make the cut.

SANDER

Combining the compactness of a sanding block with the efficiency of a power sander, the orbital palm sander quickly smooths the beveled edges of a raised panel.

Even before the invention of power tools, sanding played an integral role in the process of transforming raw wood into finished furniture. In the 18th Century, for example, English cabinetmakers fashioned their own abrasives by bonding particles of flint, quartz and volcanic pumice to parchment with hide glue. Following a more natural approach, some of their contemporaries relied on sharkskin to smooth wood.

While today's woodworkers may marvel at such painstaking sanding techniques, the process of smoothing wood has in some ways remained unchanged over the past 300 years. Sanding a piece of furniture today, as in Queen Anne's London, still consists of three distinct stages, which must be followed to ensure a perfect finish. First, the marks and blemishes left by saws, planes and other cutting and shaping tools are removed. Then the wood surfaces are carefully smoothed to accept a finish. And finally, each intermediate finish coat is abraded before the final coat is applied. Typically, each step in the sequence is peformed with a finer grade—or grit—of sandpaper, diminishing the abrasive effect of the paper until the final sanding does little more than dull the gloss of the previous finish coat.

In spite of the important role played by sanding, it is often regarded as drudgery and is given less attention than it needs. Yet no stain or finish can mask a hastily performed sanding job. Usually, they only tend to highlight it instead.

This section of the book features three types of sanders: the belt sander, the orbital sander and the random-orbit sander. Belt sanders are generally used to level stock and eliminate flaws on wood surfaces. Their powerful motors, rigid metal platens and relatively coarse sanding belts make them well suited for the first stage of sanding. The orbital and random-orbit sanders are both capable of removing blemishes from stock, but their main purpose is to prepare surfaces for finishing. With their soft sanding pads that rotate in rapid, elliptical orbits and fine-grade sanding disks, they are ideal for this task. The random-orbit sander will even remove scratches and swirl marks made by the belt or orbital sander, leaving a uniformly smooth surface.

The quality of the finish on a piece of furniture will only be as good as the care taken in sanding the surface. Here, a belt sander begins the process of smoothing a hardwood panel.

ANATOMY OF A SANDER

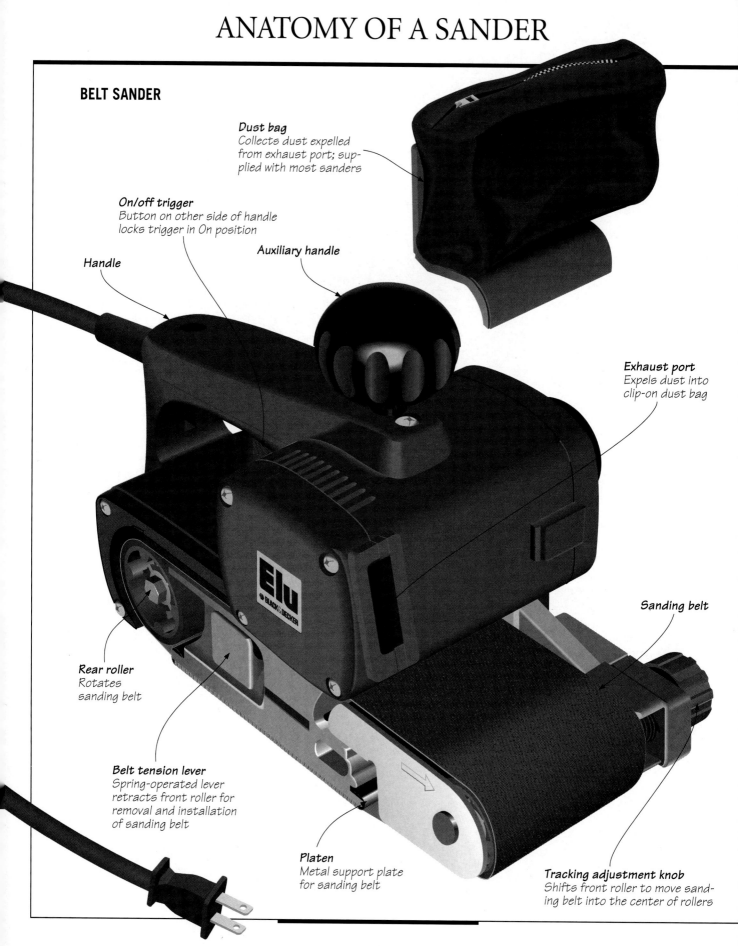

BELT SANDER

Dust bag
Collects dust expelled from exhaust port; supplied with most sanders

On/off trigger
Button on other side of handle locks trigger in On position

Auxiliary handle

Handle

Exhaust port
Expels dust into clip-on dust bag

Sanding belt

Rear roller
Rotates sanding belt

Belt tension lever
Spring-operated lever retracts front roller for removal and installation of sanding belt

Platen
Metal support plate for sanding belt

Tracking adjustment knob
Shifts front roller to move sanding belt into the center of rollers

USING SANDPAPER

GRIT	USES
60, 80	Preliminary surfacing of rough stock; levels deep scratches
100, 120	Initial smoothing of stock; levels shallow depressions and scratches
150, 180	Final smoothing of stock; prepares surfaces for finishing
220, 240	Light sanding of primer or sealer coats
280, 320	Removing air bubbles between coats of finish
360, 400, 600	Fine sanding to remove flaws before applying final coat of lacquer

Choosing sandpaper

For most finishing jobs, you should prepare the surface of your stock with papers from the grit categories shown in the chart at left. Start with a paper up to 80 grit for leveling a surface and aggressively removing stock. Move to a grit between 100 and 180 for smoothing. Use finer papers for sanding between finish coats. When buying sandpaper, consider its composition. Aluminum oxide paper is best for use with a belt sander. For grits above 150 with an orbital sander, garnet paper is the ideal. The hardest and sharpest abrasive material—silicon carbide—is recommended in grits above 220 for finish sanding with an orbital sander. Buy closed-coat paper for sanding hardwood and open-coat paper for softwood. The abrasive particles in open-coat paper are spaced farther apart, reducing clogging.

SETTING UP A SANDER

Changing a sanding belt

Set the sander on its side, then pull the belt tension lever all the way out and slip the old belt off the rollers; slide a new belt in place *(right, above)*. To avoid tearing a belt, refer to the arrows marked on the inside of the belt to orient it in the direction that the rollers revolve (some tools feature a directional arrow marked on the tool next to the front roller). Center the sandpaper on the drums, then push the tension lever back in place to lock the belt in position. To adjust the belt tracking, hold the sander upside down and switch it on. Turn the tracking adjustment knob as the belt rotates until the abrasive loop is centered on the front roller *(right, below)*.

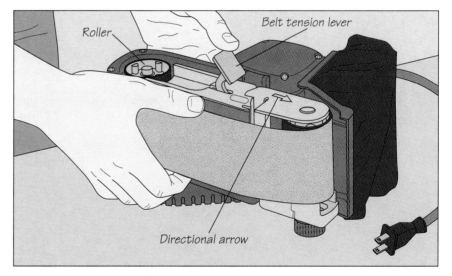

Roller

Belt tension lever

Directional arrow

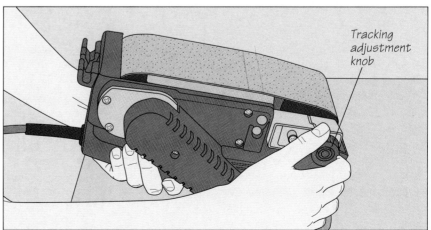

Tracking adjustment knob

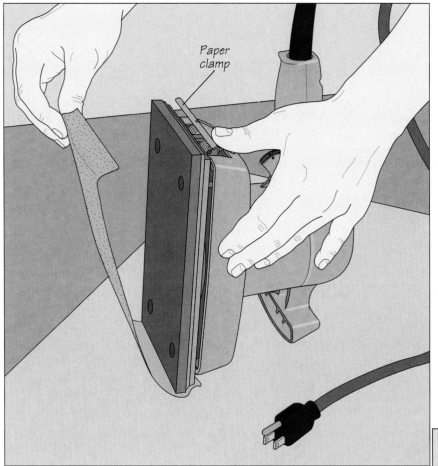

Paper
clamp

Changing sandpaper on an orbital sander
Stand the tool on end and retract one of
the paper clamps to free one end of the
sheet; then remove the other end. To
install a new sheet, retract a clamp and
fold one end of the paper over the edge
of the platen and tuck it under the clamp.
Release the clamp to lock the sheet in
place. Making certain that the paper is cov-
ering the platen completely, pull the other
end taut *(left)* and clamp it in position.

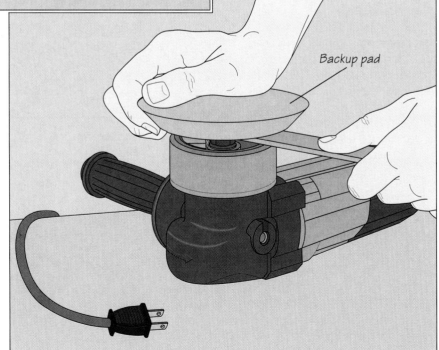

Backup pad

**Removing the backup pad from
a random-orbit sander**
The backup pad of a random-orbit sander
may need to be removed to install a finishing accessory in its place. Set the
sander upside down on a work surface.
Fit the wrench supplied with the tool
around the motor shaft between the pad
and the body of the sander, then turn the
pad counterclockwise to loosen it *(right)*.

BELT SANDER

A belt sander can perform two types of smoothing operations, depending on its orientation to the wood grain. At a 45° angle to the grain, it will remove stock quickly from a surface; running parallel to the grain, the tool will smooth even the roughest board.

Whatever the operation, clamp or nail stop blocks to your work surface to keep the workpiece from moving. Use straight, smooth, overlapping strokes, and avoid sweeping the sander in a circular pattern. To prevent gouges or rounded edges, do not turn on the sander while it sits on the workpiece. Instead, start the tool above the surface and gently lay the belt on the stock, never allowing more than one-half its length to run off the end or edge of the workpiece.

For removing stock, no tool is as effective as a belt sander. Here, it smooths the surface of a rough mahogany board.

FACE AND EDGE SANDING

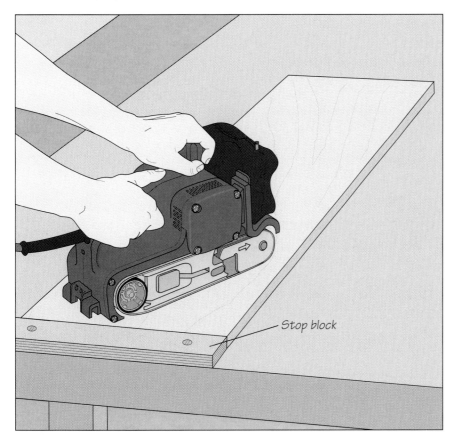

Stop block

Sanding a board

To remove stock quickly, set the sander flat on the surface at a 45° angle to the grain of the wood at one end of the workpiece *(left)*. Move the sander forward immediately. Once the tool reaches the edge of the board, pull it back, overlapping your forward stroke by one-half the width of the belt. To smooth the surface, use the same method, but this time, work with the sander parallel to the grain, as shown in the photo above.

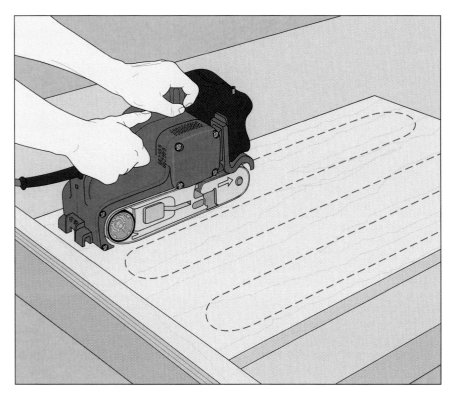

Sanding a panel

Starting at one edge of the panel, make a pass along the stock as you would when sanding a board *(page 129)*. Shift the sander over by one-half the width of the belt and pull the tool back toward you. Continue sanding back and forth, following a U-shaped pattern as shown in the illustration.

BUILD IT YOURSELF

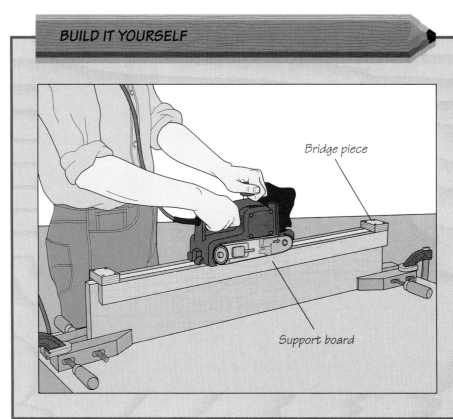

Bridge piece

Support board

EDGE-SANDING GUIDE

It can be tricky keeping a belt sander perfectly level while sanding a board edge, but the jig shown at left solves the problem. Cut two support boards from ¾-inch stock to about the length of your workpiece. Then saw bridge pieces and nail them to the support boards leaving a gap equal to the thickness of the workpiece.

To use the jig, secure the workpiece in handscrews as shown, then position the jig on the edge. Move the sander along the edge of the workpiece following the wood grain. Smooth the portions of the edge that are covered by the bridge pieces with a sanding block.

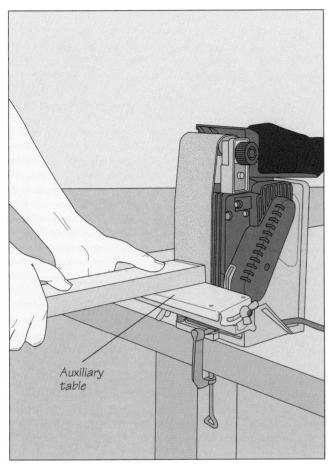

Auxiliary table

Stop block

Sanding a mitered corner
To avoid the scratches created by sanding stock against the grain, smooth the boards that meet at a mitered corner in two steps. First, sand one of the boards with the grain, sanding the other board against the grain at the same time. Then make a pass on the second board; this time avoiding contact with the first board. Slide the tool diagonally toward the outside edge of the second board, lifting it off the stock as it reaches the joint between the boards *(above)*.

Sanding a board end
Install your belt sander in a commercial bench stand or the shop-built equivalent *(page 132)*, then secure the device to a work surface. Draw a line with a combination square at the end of the workpiece to mark the point where you want the sanding to stop. Turn on the tool. Holding the workpiece with both hands, rest it flat on the stand's auxiliary table. Slowly advance the board until the end touches the belt, keeping your hands clear of the sandpaper *(above)*. Apply only moderate pressure; let the belt do the work. For a smooth finish, flip the board over several times during the operation. Sand up to the marked line on the workpiece.

SHOP TIP

Cleaning sandpaper belts
You can remove built-up sawdust and loose abrasive grit from sanding belts with a block of neoprene rubber or an old running shoe with a natural rubber sole. Set the sander on its side and lock the motor on. Hold the piece of rubber against the rotating belt for a few seconds. The dust and grit will rub off onto the rubber.

BELT SANDER STAND

To sand the ends and edges of a workpiece as well as mitered and beveled surfaces, mount your belt sander in a shop-built stand. The setup will free your hands to control stock as you feed it into the sanding belt. The stand shown at right is customized for the model of sander in the illustration. The dimensions of your jig will depend on the size of your tool.

Cut the base and the raised table from ¾-inch plywood. The base should be large enough to hold the sander and the table. Next, cut the support posts to fit in the handles of the sander. Set the tool on its side on the jig and slip the posts in place, then screw them to the base. Screw the raised table in place, with its edge just clear of the sanding belt. Check that the belt is parallel to the raised table. Turn on the tool and make sure that it operates smoothly without moving about in the jig.

Clamp the stand to a work surface and set the sander in place. To sand the mitered end shown, secure a stop block to the raised table at the same angle as the miter. The block will help you hold the mitered end parallel to the sanding belt. Lock the sander's trigger in the On position. To sand the workpiece, follow the same procedure you would use for a square end *(page 131)*, keeping the edge of the board butted against the stop block.

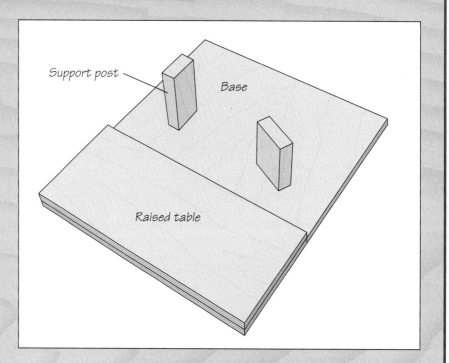

Support post

Base

Raised table

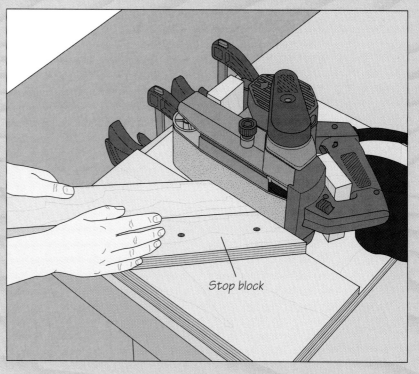

Stop block

Gang sanding

To smooth the edges of several work-pieces of the same width, sand them together in a single operation known as gang sanding. Place the stock face to face and align their ends, then secure them with handscrews and clamps. Working with the grain, sand the pieces just as though they were a single board.

SHOP TIP

Sanding a circular workpiece
To keep circular stock from moving as you smooth its surface with a belt sander, secure it in a V-shaped stop block. Make the jig from a piece of plywood that is thinner than your workpiece, and roughly the width of the circle's diameter. Cut out a wedge large enough to hold the stock. Clamp the jig to a work surface and place the workpiece in the wedge so you can work parallel with the grain. Sand the workpiece the same way you would a panel (page 130).

BUILD IT YOURSELF

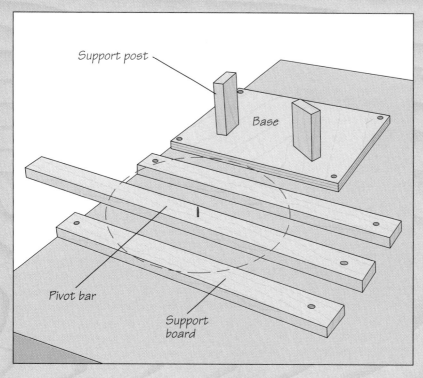

Support post

Base

Pivot bar

Support
board

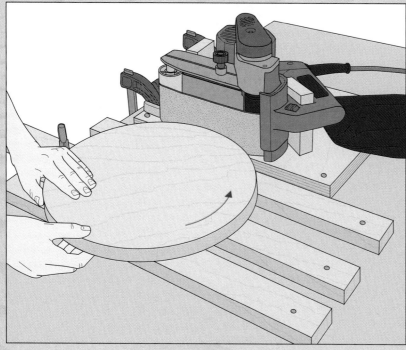

CIRCLE-SANDING JIG

The jig shown at left will allow you to smooth the edges of a circular workpiece with a belt sander in a uniform and controlled fashion. The dimensions of the jig will depend on the size of your sander.

Make the base and the support posts the same way as a sander stand *(page 132)*, but without the raised table. Use 1-by-2 stock for the support boards and the pivot bar, cutting the boards longer than the diameter of your workpiece and making the bar longer than the boards. Screw the boards to the work surface so they will support the workpiece near its circumference.

Drive a nail through the middle of the pivot bar and press it into the center of the underside of the stock. Flip the two pieces over and screw one end of the pivot bar to the work surface midway between the support boards, leaving the screw loose enough to allow you to pivot the bar's other end.

To use the jig, set the sander in place on the base, fitting the support posts through the tool's handles. Turn on the sander and, if necessary, readjust the tracking to move the belt down to the jig base; lock the trigger. To sand the workpiece, pull the free end of the pivot bar toward the sander until the stock touches the sanding belt. Clamp the free end of the bar to the work surface. Then rotate the workpiece steadily against the direction of belt rotation until the edge is smooth, periodically shifting the pivot bar toward the sander.

ORBITAL SANDER

Its pad moving in tight circles at up to 12,000 orbits per minute, the orbital sander excels at producing silky smooth surfaces. Here, it prepares a frame-and-panel door for a coat of finish.

Orbital sanders are sometimes called "finish sanders" because they are ideal for smoothing surfaces between finish coats. But their fast and tight orbiting movements (the sanding pad moves only $\frac{1}{16}$ to $\frac{3}{32}$ inch with each stroke), make them equally handy for knocking down edges or smoothing wood prior to finishing. In fact, two-handed and palm orbital sanders do most of the sanding in many woodworking shops.

The orbital sander's single drawback is its tendency to leave swirl marks on a surface. These are actually dozens of tiny spiral scratches in the wood. To avoid such imperfections, use high quality paper. Do not skip grades when moving to a finer paper, and set the sander down on your workpiece gently when you start a job. To remove any remaining swirl marks, use a sanding block.

FACE AND EDGE SANDING

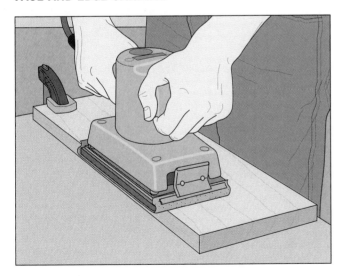

Sanding a board face
After clamping the board to a work surface, hold the sander above it and turn on the tool. Bring the sander gently down onto the wood surface parallel to the grain at one end of the board. Move the tool forward, applying light downward pressure *(above)*. Do not let the sander rest in one place. At the end of the board, pull the sander back, overlapping your forward stroke. Continue in this manner until you cover the entire surface. To avoid rounding the edges of your stock, do not let more than one-half of the platen extend off the workpiece.

Cardboard

Paper clamp handle

Sanding inside a carcase
Smooth the interior surfaces of a carcase the same way you would sand a board *(step left)*. To avoid marring adjoining panels with protruding parts of the sander such as the paper clamp handles, place a sheet of cardboard up against the vertical surfaces *(above)*.

Orbital
palm
sander

Rounding edges and ends

Holding your stock securely on the work surface, grip an orbital palm sander firmly and turn it on. Set the tool on the end of the workpiece at a 45° angle and move it back and forth until the end or edge is rounded to your satisfaction. For best results, make a series of passes with progressively finer-grit sandpaper.

SHOP TIP

Making a polishing pad

Most orbital sanders can be outfitted with various polishing and buffing accessories. You can make your own polishing pad by folding sheets of cheesecloth into a pad several layers thick. Install the cheesecloth on the sander as you would a sheet of sandpaper, making sure that the pad is taut and covers the platen completely.

SANDING IN TIGHT SPOTS

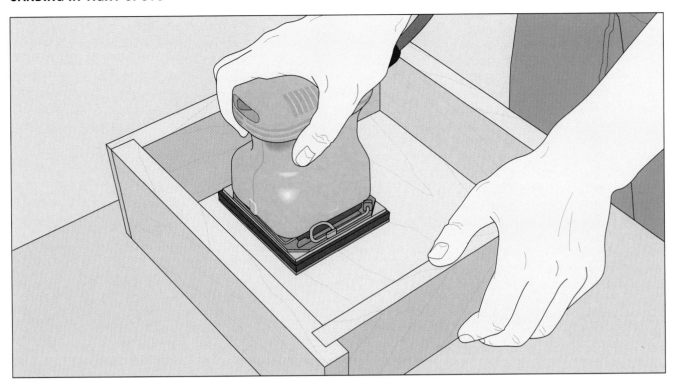

Sanding in a drawer

An orbital palm sander is your best bet for smoothing interior surfaces in confined areas, such as small drawers. To sand the drawer bottom, hold the piece steady on a work surface and turn on the tool. Set the sander flat on the drawer bottom at one corner, then move it along the surface in overlapping, parallel strokes until the surface is smooth *(above)*. Ride the edges of the sander along the drawer sides; the design of the palm sander will enable you to sand right up to the adjoining surfaces.

SHOP TIP

The corner sander

For smoothing surfaces in tight spots such as corners and rabbets, use the corner sander. It operates like an orbital sander, but has a 3-inch-wide triangular sanding pad instead of a rectangular one. The pad can be rotated to any position relative to the body of the sander. Specially designed triangular sanding sheets, from 40 to 120 grit, are available for the tool. They are fastened with either the hook-and-loop or the PSA system, depending on the model.

RANDOM-ORBIT SANDER

Standard equipment in auto body shops for many years, the random-orbit sander has recently found a well-deserved home in woodworking shops. This tool's ability to remove stock quickly while leaving the surface underneath relatively scratch- and swirl-free makes it a good choice for many jobs. Its rapid, random orbits are good for removing old finishes from an antique or buffing final coats of lacquer. The tool's round backup pad also makes it ideal for sanding contoured and curved surfaces.

For best results, keep the sanding disk flat on the surface while you are sanding. Follow the direction of the wood grain, moving the sander in a circular pattern. When polishing a surface with the sander, avoid excessive downward pressure; the pad should "float" over the finish. And remember to use the sander's lowest speed setting; high-speed buffing tends to wipe off the finish.

The random-orbit sander is an ideal choice for smoothing the rails and stiles of a tongue-and-groove door. Because its sanding pad rotates in random orbits, the tool does not leave swirl marks or scratches when sanding against the grain.

CONTOUR SANDING

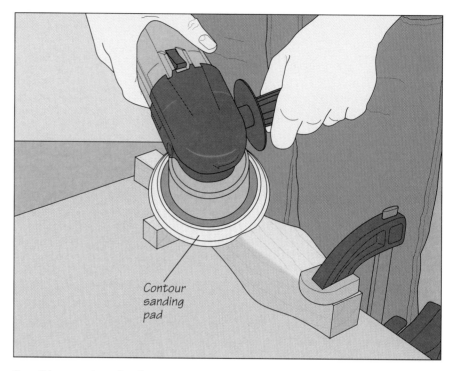

Contour sanding pad

Smoothing a contoured surface

Clamp your stock to a work surface. Remove the backup pad from the sander *(page 128)* and replace it with a contour sanding pad; install a sanding disk. Holding the tool with both hands above the workpiece, turn it on and lower the pad onto the surface. Apply moderate downward pressure while you move the sander back and forth along the workpiece until the surface is smooth; reposition any clamps and turn the workpiece as necessary.

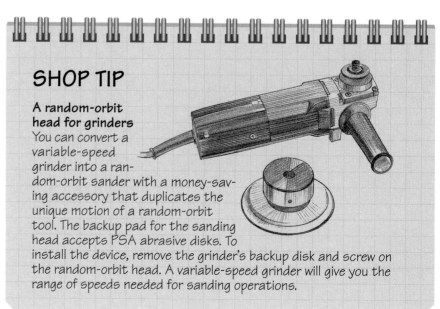

SHOP TIP

A random-orbit head for grinders
You can convert a variable-speed grinder into a random-orbit sander with a money-saving accessory that duplicates the unique motion of a random-orbit tool. The backup pad for the sanding head accepts PSA abrasive disks. To install the device, remove the grinder's backup disk and screw on the random-orbit head. A variable-speed grinder will give you the range of speeds needed for sanding operations.

POLISHING

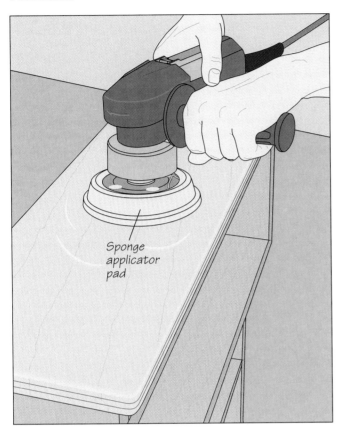

Sponge applicator pad

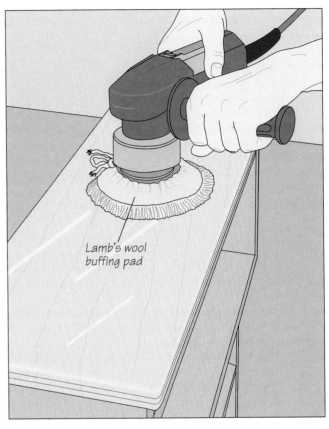

Lamb's wool buffing pad

Buffing a finished surface

Clean the surface to remove all dust and make sure that it is dry. Smear a thin layer of paste wax over the surface by hand. Remove the backup pad from the sander *(page 128)* and install a sponge applicator pad. Set the sander to its lowest speed and turn it on. Lower the pad onto the surface and move the sander back and forth along the surface, applying light pressure to spread the wax evenly *(above, left)*. Once the surface has a smooth and uniform luster, replace the sponge applicator pad with the sander's backup pad, then install a lamb's wool buffing pad. Switch on the tool again and repeat the procedure to obtain a bright and uniform shine *(above, right)*.

SHOP TIP

Steadying a work-piece with under-padding
To keep a small work-piece steady while smoothing its surface with a random-orbit sander, set it on an old piece of carpet underpadding. The foam rubber will anchor the stock to your work surface, keeping the workpiece from moving as the sander does its work.

GLOSSARY

A-B

Bevel cut: Sawing at an angle from face to face along the length or width of a workpiece.

Biscuit: A thin oval-shaped wafer of compressed wood, usually beech, which fits into a semicircular slot cut by a plate joiner.

Biscuit joint: *See plate joint.*

Biscuit pucker: A blistering of the surface of a workpiece caused by inserting biscuits too close to the surface of the stock.

Brad-point bit: A drill bit featuring a sharpened centerpoint and two cutting spurs on its circumference.

C

Cabriole leg: A type of furniture leg characterized by rounded contours designed to imitate the graceful leg of a leaping animal.

Carbide-tipped blade: A saw blade on which the teeth are made of a compound of carbon and steel; such blade edges are stronger and stay sharper longer than conventional high-speed steel blades.

Carcase: A box-like construction that makes up the body of a piece of furniture.

Chamfer: A decorative bevel cut along the edge of a workpiece.

Chuck: Adjustable jaws on a drill for holding bits or other cutting or sanding accessories.

Collet: The sleeve on a router that holds the shank of a bit.

Combination blade: A circular saw blade designed for making both crosscuts and rip cuts.

Compound cut: Sawing through a board with the blade presented at angles other than 90° relative to the face and edge of the stock.

Counterbore bit: An adjustable combination bit for the electric drill that bores a pilot hole, clearance hole, countersinking hole and counterbore hole in one operation.

Contour cut: Sawing along a curved line, usually with a saber saw.

Countersink: Drilling a hole that permits the head of a screw or bolt to lie flush with or slightly below a wood surface.

Crosscut: Sawing across the wood grain of a workpiece.

D-E

Dado: A rectangular channel cut into a workpiece.

Direction of feed: The direction that a tool is fed into a workpiece when making a cut.

Dovetail joint: A method of joining wood at corners by means of interlocking pins and tails; the name derives from the distinctive shape cut into the ends of joining boards.

Dowel: A wood pin used to reinforce certain types of joints.

Dowel center: A metal cylinder that is inserted into a dowel hole to pinpoint a matching hole in a mating workpiece.

Drop-foot: A type of circular saw on which the depth of cut is changed by moving the entire saw up and down relative to its shoe. *See pivot-foot.*

Edge gluing: Bonding several boards together edge-to-edge to form a solid panel.

End grain: The arrangement and direction of the wood fibers running across the width of a workpiece when viewed from the ends.

F-G

Featherboard: A piece of wood cut with fingers or "feathers" at one end; used in conjunction with clamps to hold a workpiece against the fence or table of a power tool.

Fence: An adjustable guide designed to keep the edge or face of a workpiece a set distance from the cutting edge of a tool.

Forstner bit: A drill bit with a razor rim and cutters for boring flat-bottomed holes.

Grain: The arrangement and direction of the fibers that make up wood.

Grit: The concentration of abrasive particles on a piece of sandpaper or sanding disk.

Grooving blade: A plate joiner blade that cuts continuous grooves.

Gullet: The gap between teeth on a saw blade.

H-I-J-K-L

Hardwood: Wood cut from deciduous (leaf-shedding) trees; some types may actually be soft and easy to cut.

Hook-and-loop disk: A sanding or polishing disk with a Velcro™ backing; used with random orbit-sanders.

Jig: Device for guiding a tool or holding a workpiece in position.

Jointing: Cutting thin shavings from the edge of a workpiece until it is flat and square to the face.

Kerf: A cut made in wood by the thickness of a saw blade.

Kerf splitter: A device that holds a kerf slightly open during a cut to prevent the saw blade from binding.

Kickback: The tendency of a workpiece to be thrown back in the direction of the operator of a power tool.

M-N-O

Miter cut: A cut that angles across the face of a workpiece.

Miter gauge: A device that slides in a slot on the table of a power tool, providing support for the workpiece as it is fed into the bit or blade.

Molding: Decorative strips of wood that can be carved on a router.

Mortise: A rectangular or oval-shaped hole cut into a piece of wood.

Mortise-and-tenon joint: A joinery technique in which a projecting tenon on one board fits into a mortise on another.

Orbital action: The up-and-forward movement of some saber saw blades on their upstroke; replaces the traditional straight up-and-down action of a reciprocating-type saber saw. Also, the eccentric rotation of the abrasive disk on an orbital or random-orbit sander.

P-Q

Pilot hole: A hole bored into a workpiece to prepare for insertion of a screw; usually made slightly smaller than the threaded part of the screw.

Pivot-foot: A circular saw with a depth-of-cut adjustment that is made by pivoting the saw up and down at a point near the front of the saw. *See drop-foot.*

Plate joint: A method of joining wood in which biscuits of wood fit into slots cut in mating boards.

Plunge cut: A cut by a saw blade into the interior of a workpiece without slicing in from the edge of the stock.

Pressure-sensitive adhesive (PSA) disk: A sandpaper disk with an adhesive backing: for use with random-orbit and orbital sanders; available in different grits.

Push block or stick: A device used to feed a workpiece into the bit or blade of a tool to protect the fingers of the operator.

R

Rabbet: A step-like cut in the edge or end of a board; usually forms part of a joint.

Release cut: A preliminary incision from the edge of a workpiece to a line about to be cut; such preparations allow a saber saw to cut along tighter turns by facilitating the removal of waste wood.

Rip cut: A cut that follows the grain of a workpiece—usually made along its length.

S-T-U-V-W-X-Y-Z

Scrolling saber saw: A saber saw that features a blade that rotates 360° for easier cutting of tight curves.

Shoe: The metal base on a saber saw or circular saw, which rests on a workpiece during a cut.

Softwood: Wood cut from logs of cone-bearing (coniferous) trees.

Spade bit: A flat drill bit for boring holes up to 1½ inches in diameter.

Spline: A small piece of wood that fits in mating grooves in two workpieces; serves to reinforce the joint between them.

Stop collar: An electric drill accessory that fits around a bit to stop a drilling operation at a certain depth.

Stopped hole: A hole that does not pass all the way through a workpiece; also known as a blind hole.

Stopped rabbet: A rabbet that does not run the full length or width of a workpiece.

Taper cut: An angled cut along the length of a workpiece that reduces its width at one end.

Tearout: The tendency of a blade or bit to tear the fibers of the wood it is cutting, leaving ragged edges on the workpiece; a problem especially when making dado cuts.

Three-wing slotting cutter: A piloted groove-cutting router bit.

Tenon: A protrusion from the end of a board; fits into a mortise.

Torque: The twisting force of a drill or router bit as it rotates in the tool.

INDEX

Page references in *italics* indicate
an illustration of subject matter.
Page references in **bold** indicate
a Build It Yourself project.

ACKNOWLEDGMENTS

The editors wish to thank the following:

CIRCULAR SAW
Adjustable Clamp Co., Chicago, IL; American Tool Cos., Lincoln, NE; Delta International Machinery/Porter Cable, Guelph, Ont.; Dewalt Industrial Tool Co., Hampstead, MD; Griset Industries, Inc., Santa Ana, CA; Makita Canada, Inc., Whitby, Ont.; Sandvik Saws and Tools Co., Scranton, PA; Sears, Roebuck and Co., Chicago, IL; Skil Power Tools Canada, Markham, Ont.; Stanley Tools, Division of the Stanley Works, New Britain, CT; Vermont American Corp., Lincolnton, NC and Louisville, KY

SABER SAW
Adjustable Clamp Co., Chicago, IL; American Tool Cos., Lincoln, NE; Delta International Machinery/Porter Cable, Guelph, Ont.; Dewalt Industrial Tool Co., Hampstead, MD; Hitachi Power Tools U.S.A. Ltd., Norcross, GA; Robert Bosch Power Tools Inc., (Canada) Mississauga, Ont.; Rule Industries, Burlington, MA; Sears, Roebuck and Co., Chicago, IL; Skil Power Tools Canada, Markham, Ont.; Stanley Tools, Division of the Stanley Works, New Britain, CT; Vermont American Corp., Lincolnton, NC and Louisville, KY

ELECTRIC DRILL
Adjustable Clamp Co., Chicago, IL; American Tool Cos., Lincoln, NE; Black and Decker Power Tools, Hunt Valley, MD; Delta International Machinery/Porter Cable, Guelph, Ont.; Dewalt Industrial Tool Co., Hampstead, MD; Griset Industries, Inc., Santa Ana, CA; Lee Valley Tools Ltd., Ottawa, Ont.; Leichtung Workshops, Cleveland, OH; Makita Canada, Inc., Whitby, Ont.; Robert Bosch Power Tools Inc., (Canada) Mississauga, Ont.; Sandvik Saws and Tools Co., Scranton, PA; Sears, Roebuck and Co., Chicago, IL; Skil Power Tools Canada, Markham, Ont.; Stanley Tools, Division of the Stanley Works, New Britain, CT; Tru-Align Manufacturing Inc., Tempe, AZ; Veritas Tools Inc., Ottawa, Ont./Ogdensburg, NY; Vermont American Corp., Lincolnton, NC and Louisville, KY

ROUTER
Adjustable Clamp Co., Chicago, IL; American Tool Cos., Lincoln, NE; Black and Decker/Elu Power Tools, Hunt Valley, MD; Delta International Machinery/Porter Cable, Guelph, Ont.; Freud Westmore Tools, Ltd., Mississauga, Ont.; Griset Industries, Inc., Santa Ana, CA; Hitachi Power Tools U.S.A. Ltd., Norcross, GA; Leigh Industries Ltd., Port Coquitlam, BC; Linemaster Switch, Corp., Woodstock, CT; Makita Canada, Inc., Whitby, Ont.; Oak Park Enterprises, Ltd., Elie, Man.; Robert Bosch Power Tools Inc., (Canada) Mississauga, Ont.; Sandvik Saws and Tools Co., Scranton, PA; Sears, Roebuck and Co., Chicago, IL; Shopsmith, Inc., Montreal, Que.; Stanley Tools, Division of the Stanley Works, New Britain, CT; Taylor Design Group, Inc., Dallas, TX

PLATE JOINER
Adjustable Clamp Co., Chicago, IL; American Tool Cos., Lincoln, NE; Black and Decker/Elu Power Tools, Hunt Valley, MD; Delta International Machinery/Porter Cable, Guelph, Ont.; Stanley Tools, Division of the Stanley Works, New Britain, CT; Steiner-Lamello A.G. Switzerland/Colonial Saw Co., Kingston, MA

SANDER
Adjustable Clamp Co., Chicago, IL; American Tool Cos., Lincoln, NE; Black and Decker/Elu Power Tools, Hunt Valley, MD; Delta International Machinery/Porter Cable, Guelph, Ont.; Dewalt Industrial Tool Co., Hampstead, MD; Fein Canadian Power Tool Company (Que). Ltd., Montreal, Que.; Hitachi Power Tools U.S.A. Ltd., Norcross, GA; Marshco Products, Brooks, ME; Robert Bosch Power Tools Inc., (Canada) Mississauga, Ont.; Sears, Roebuck and Co., Chicago, IL; 3M Canada Inc., Dorval, Que.

The following persons also assisted in the preparation
of this book:

Renaud Boisjoly, Jean-Pierre Bourgeois, Lorraine Doré, Dominique Gagné, Graphor Consultation, Christiane L'Italien, Gérard Mariscalchi, James Thérien, Jocelyn Veillette

PICTURE CREDITS

Cover Robert Chartier
6-7, 8-9, 10-11 Ian Gittler